Test Your Professional English

Business: Intermediate

Steve Flinders

Series Editor: Nick Brieger

Pearson Education Limited
Edinburgh Gate
Harlow
Essex CM20 2JE, England
and Associated Companies throughout the world.

ISBN 0 582 45149 3

First published 1997 under the title Test Your Business English: Intermediate
This edition published 2002
Text copyright © Steve Flinders 1997, 2002

Designed and typeset by Pantek Arts Ltd, Maidstone, Kent
Test Your format devised by Peter Watcyn-Jones
Illustrations by Roger Fereday and Anthony Seldon
Printed in Italy by Rotolito Lombarda

Acknowledgements
Many thanks to John Fagan and Bob Dignen at York Associates for their advice on the content of this edition, and to Mathieu, Jérôme and Lorenza for their help with the Answers and the Word list.

Published by Pearson Education Limited in association with Penguin Books Ltd, both companies being subsidiaries of Pearson plc.

For a complete list of the titles available from Penguin English please visit our website at www.penguinenglish.com, or write to your local Pearson Education office or to: Marketing Department, Penguin Longman Publishing, 80 Strand, London WC2R 0RL.

Contents

Section 8 Business in the twenty-first century

To the student

Do you work in business and use English in your job? Or are you a business student? Whatever your background, if you need to improve your business English, the tests in this book will help. Designed to accompany *Test Your Professional English: Business General*, they will check your knowledge of more business words and essential business expressions so that you can understand and communicate more effectively and confidently.

There are eight sections in the book. The first section tests your ability to talk about yourself and your background: to say who you are and talk about your business role and experience. The other seven sections each cover a different aspect of business – from business language and communication to business in the twenty-first century. You can work through the book from beginning to end or you can work first on the tests which are most important to you.

Many tests also have tips (advice) on language and language learning, and information about business. Do read these explanations and tips: they are there to help you.

To make the book more challenging and more fun, many different kinds of test are used, including gap-filling, word families, multiple choice and crosswords. There is a key at the back of the book so that you can check your answers, and a word list to help you revise key vocabulary.

Your vocabulary is an essential resource for effective communication. It is important to remember that the more words you know, the more you can say and the more you can understand. These tests can help you check what you know and develop your knowledge of new concepts and terms in a structured and systematic way. This book can help you significantly increase your business vocabulary.

Steve Flinders

The full series consists of:

Test Your Professional English: Accounting	Alison Pohl
Test Your Professional English: Business General	Steve Flinders
Test Your Professional English: Business Intermediate	Steve Flinders
Test Your Professional English: Finance	Simon Sweeney
Test Your Professional English: Hotel and Catering	Alison Pohl
Test Your Professional English: Law	Nick Brieger
Test Your Professional English: Management	Simon Sweeney
Test Your Professional English: Marketing	Simon Sweeney
Test Your Professional English: Medical	Alison Pohl
Test Your Professional English: Secretarial	Alison Pohl

1 Your interview

Complete the interview questions with words from the box.

achievement	approach	get	good	know	learn
like	look for	motivates	offer	plan	sort
strengths	~~tell~~	weaknesses	work		

1   _____*Tell*_____ me about yourself.

2   Why should we _____ you the job?

3   What is your major _____?

4   What are you _____ at?

5   What _____ of person are you?

6   What are your _____ and _____?

7   What do you _____ about our organization?

8   How would you _____ this job?

9   How do you _____ things done?

10   What do you _____ in a manager?

11   What _____ you?

12   Do you like to _____ in a team or on your own?

13   What do you _____ best about your current job?

14   What did you _____ in your last job?

15   How long would you _____ to stay with this company?

Here are some other questions you can prepare to ask or answer in a job interview:

How important is work to you?
What sort of salary are you expecting?
What will you do if you don't get this job?
What decisions do you find it easy to make? difficult to make?

2 Your education

Marcia Garcia tells us about her educational background. Complete each sentence with one of the words or phrases from the box below. You will need to put the verbs into the right tense. (You can then make similar sentences about your own education and qualifications – academic and professional.)

apply	degree	graduate (verb)	grant	higher degree
	job	option	PhD	place	~~primary school~~
	thesis	secondary school	stay on	study	subject

1   I started at ___*primary school*___ in London when I was five.

2   At the age of 11, I went on to _____ , also in London.

3   At 17, I _____ to university.

4   I got a _____ at Manchester to _____ Engineering.

5   But at the end of the first year I changed to another _____ .

6   I _____ from university in 1997.

7   I have a first-class _____ in Economics.

8   I decided to _____ at university.

9   So I did a _____ in Business Administration at the University of California.

10   During the course, I did an _____ on small business development.

11   I found the topic so interesting that I applied for a
_____ to do a doctorate on the same subject.

12   Once I had got the money, I had to write a 50,000-word
_____ .

13   So now I have a BA, an MBA and a _____ .

14   All I need now is a _____ !

People who do well in their **examinations** ('exams') at school or at
university usually have good **academic qualifications**. In Britain and the
USA, the most common university **qualifications** are a BA (Bachelor of Arts)
or BSc (Bachelor of Science) after three years and an MA (Master of Arts) or
MSc (Master of Science) after another one or two years. Many people in
business also have some kind of **professional qualification** and for some
jobs you must have such a qualification.
When students get **grants** from the government, they keep the money.
When they get **loans**, they have to pay the money back later.
A **PhD** is a Doctor of Philosophy. Doctors of Medicine are **MDs**.

3 Your experience

Charlie Kim tells us about his professional history up to now. Complete the sentences with verbs from the box. Make sure the verbs are in the right tense.

> buy   ~~drop out~~   join   look after   move   promote   run
>
> sell   set up   spend   take off   write

1 I went to college in the States but got bored so I _**dropped out**_ after two years without a degree.

2 I _____ a company making computer games.

3 After six months I was _____ to the post of chief games designer.

4 I _____ two years there learning the business.

5 Then I _____ to a bigger games company for more money but I hated it.

6 So I decided to _____ my own company.

7 With my partner, Mario Carter, I co-_____ the software for a game called *Sudden Death*.

8 It _____ a million copies in its first year.

9 We _____ another games company in Japan with the money we made.

10 Now I _____ the company in the States.

11 And Mario _____ the company in Japan.

12 Now I'd like to _____ a year _____ to learn about website design.

'He says he wants his own company but he wants to get some work experience with us first.'

Fewer people today think they will have **lifetime employment** with the same company. Companies are quicker to **let** people **go** and so people **change jobs** more often.

4 Your job

Match the names and titles (1–11) with the job descriptions (a–k).

1	**Charley Simpson** **Civil Engineer**	**a**	We have two teams calling possible clients to fix meetings with the reps.
2	**Sarah Whitaker** **General Practitioner**	**b**	We try to adapt our courses to the needs of each individual learner.
3	**Sidney Mole** **Bank Manager**	**c**	We deal with most users' problems by phone.
4	**Mary Somerville** **Management Consultant**	**d**	I have the biology chair.
5	**Professor Alan Stevens**	**e**	We do mainly children's titles and dictionaries.
6	**Rosemary Mell** **Publisher**	**f**	We examine and (usually) approve company accounts.
7	**Jack Castle** **Sales Representative**	**g**	I have about 1,500 patients on my list.
8	**Sally Blunkett** **Telesales Manager**	**h**	I specialize in advising on management reporting systems.
9	**Alan Murphy** **Technical Support**	**i**	We are always ready to discuss lending possibilities with our clients.
10	**Susan Reed** **Trainer**	**j**	I visit my clients two or three times a year to tell them about our latest products.
11	**Caroline Bevan** **Auditor**	**k**	I build bridges.

Civil servants are people who work for the government, in the **civil service**. A *rep* is a sales representative. A *general practitioner* is a medical doctor. What is your job title in English? What do you reply when people ask you: 'What do you do?'. It is very important to be able to say what you do in English. Practise!

5 Your responsibilities

Sidney Carton is talking about his job responsibilities but is having problems with his prepositions. Complete the following sentences with a preposition from the box, where necessary. You need some of the prepositions more than once. Some of the sentences do not need an extra word. You can then make similar sentences about your own job responsibilities.

after	in	on	out	to	with

1 I head ⸺ the marketing department at Power Enterprises.

2 I report directly _____ Mr Power himself.

3 I look _____ a department of about 30 people.

4 I deal _____ all the major aspects of the company's marketing strategy.

5 I liaise _____ the other members of the management committee.

6 I listen carefully _____ what our customers say.

7 I handle _____ one or two of the major accounts myself.

8 I'm working _____ a very important account at the moment.

9 I also monitor _____ the general situation in the market place.

10 We carry _____ market surveys regularly.

11 We test _____ new products on groups of consumers.

12 I am also involved _____ one or two of Mr Power's takeover projects.

To talk about the person above you in the organization, you can also say:
I answer to Mr Power.

To talk about your colleagues, you can also say:
I work with Marcelle Joubert and Jesus Degas.

6 Your pay

Match each form of payment (1–11) with the right person (a–k).

1	grant	_h_	a	author
2	salary	___	b	senior manager
3	wage	___	c	laid-off employee
4	commission	___	d	government
5	fees	___	e	blue-collar worker
6	dividend	___	f	retired employee
7	royalty	___	g	sales representative
8	stock option	___	h	student
9	pension	___	i	consultant
10	tax	___	j	shareholder
11	redundancy pay	___	k	white-collar worker

Does a royal earn royalties?

7 Your pension

Juanita Hernandez has just joined Nice Cream Inc. She is reading about her pension in the documentation the Human Resources Manager gave her. Fill in the missing words from the box.

average earnings	board	bridging	brokers	contribution
contributory	early retirement	fund	holiday	lump sum
~~plan~~	portable	retire	trustees	

Welcome to Nice Cream. This sheet gives you information about your Nice Cream pension (1) _____*plan*_____ .

Your Nice Cream pension is fully (2) _____ , so if you decide to leave the company, you can take your pension with you.

The Nice Cream scheme is a (3) _____ one. This means that every month you pay a (4) _____ into the company pension (5) _____ and the company pays an equal amount. You can choose how much you pay and you can also pay into the scheme a (6) _____ of any size at any time. If the scheme has more money than it needs, you can take a contributions (7) _____ and stop paying a monthly sum for a while.

The fund is managed by a (8) _____ of (9) _____ who are appointed jointly by the senior management board of the company and your trade union representatives. This committee works completely independently of the company. The company cannot touch the money in the pension fund.

If you are a member of this scheme for 35 years, you can expect to (10) _____ at the age of 65 with a pension equal to 80% of your final (11) _____. If you take (12) _____, you can receive a (13) _____ pension until you are 65 and can receive your full pension.

We think that this scheme is one of the best available and one reason why so many people decide to stay with Nice Cream. However, if you prefer not to take part, we can give you the names of insurance and pensions (14) _____ who can give you independent advice on other products on the market.

8 Your computer

Sidney has been away for a few years. Help Greta explain to him about his new computer by selecting the right words or phrases from the box.

---

click   copy   delete   file   icons   menus   mouse   ~~personal computer~~
point   printer   save   select   spreadsheet   word processing

---

Greta: So where's the new PC?

Sidney: PC?

Greta: (1) *Personal computer*.

Sidney: Oh, it's here. But what's this thing you're moving around with your hand?

Greta: It's a (2) _____.

Sidney: A what?

Greta: Let's switch it on and go into Windows. Now, look at all these (3) _____ on the screen.

Sidney: OK.

Greta: If I (4) _____ the cursor at one of them and then double (5) _____, I can open any of them up and take a look inside.

Sidney: And what is inside?

Greta: Well, let's do a bit of (6) _____ first – that's just a way of saying you're going to create some text.

Sidney: You mean I'm going to type something.

Greta: That's right. You can open up a new (7) _____ and then you can access any of these pull-down (8) _____ like this.

Sidney: But what if I type something and make a mistake?

Greta: You can (9) _____ it like this. But it's also very important to (10) _____ everything you produce.

Sidney: And if I want to move some text from one place to another?

Greta: You (11) _____ all the text you want to move and then move it like this. And you can also (12) _____ text like this.

Sidney: And how do I get it from the screen onto paper?

Greta: Your computer is connected to a (13) _____ and so you can send a message to it from here.

Sidney: And what about figures? Can it add up?

Greta: Yes, you can go into (14) _____ software like this and create a table with columns and rows to enter figures in.

Sidney: Well, it's not bad, but can't it play any games?

9 Business verbs 1

For each of the verbs below, three of the four words or expressions fit. In each case, circle the one that does not fit.

1	DO	a) business	(b) a profit
		c) a job	d) a deal
2	MAKE	a) money	b) business
		c) a loss	d) a decision
3	TAKE	a) a long time	b) a decision
		c) appropriate measures	d) a deadline
4	HAVE	a) progress	b) something to eat
		c) shares in a company	d) a meeting
5	MEET	a) a deadline	b) customers' expectations
		c) an appointment	d) a target
6	LAUNCH	a) a product	b) a ship
		c) a campaign	d) a team
7	CUT	a) costs	b) jobs
		c) a decision	d) a price
8	CARRY OUT	a) a meeting	b) duties
		c) research	d) a market survey
9	ACHIEVE	a) progress	b) a breakthrough
		c) a job	d) little
10	REACH	a) a decision	b) a strategy
		c) an agreement	d) a target

When you've finished:
You have chosen the word or phrase that doesn't fit with each of the verbs 1–10. Can you think of a verb that does fit with each of the words or phrases that you circled?

10 Business verbs 2

Look at the verbs below and decide which one goes with which word or phrase from lists A and B, as in the example.

		A	**B**
	DRAW ~ / DRAW UP ~	a conclusion	an agenda

You draw a conclusion.

You draw up an agenda.

		A	**B**
1	open ~ / open up ~	a market	a letter
2	put forward ~ / put ~	a meeting	a question
3	~ fall / ~ fall down	share prices	trees in storms
4	fill ~ / fill in ~	a form	with pride
5	cut ~ / cut down on ~	cigarettes	costs
6	lay ~ / lay off ~	workers	foundations
7	break ~ / break up~	bad news to someone	inefficient companies
8	sell ~ / sell off ~	parts of a company	goods at a discount
9	kick ~ / kick off ~	yourself	a meeting
10	take ~ / take on ~	extra staff	too long
11	pick ~ / ~ pick up	the best person	a market can
12	bring ~ / bring up ~	a problem at a meeting	dynamism to the job
13	carry ~ / carry out ~	duties	passengers

11 Business verbs 3

Jose Spragg has just won the World Manager of the Year competition. Take a power verb (1–15) and add a sentence-ending from the column on the right (a–o) to make the sentences that the judges used to describe him.

1	He thinks	a	costs.
2	He focuses	b	organizations.
3	He motivates	c	market opportunities.
4	He overcomes	d	change.
5	He identifies	e	performance.
6	He adds	f	results.
7	He reduces	g	profits.
8	He leads	h	strategically.
9	He builds	i	people.
10	He resolves	j	winning teams.
11	He transforms	k	conflict.
12	He manages and facilitates	l	obstacles.
13	He measures	m	value.
14	He maximizes	n	on the customer.
15	He gets	o	by example.

What are the power verbs that describe you?
Would you put them in your CV?

12 Business verbs and nouns

Fit one verb from the box into each of the headlines (1–13) about Kazoulis Communications in the business press. There are three possible answers for 9.

BENDS	CUTS	~~GENERATES~~	IMPLEMENTS	INCREASES	LAUNCHES
MAKES	MEETS	PLAYS	REACHES	RUNS	SENDS	SIGNS

1 EXPANSION IN US ___GENERATES___ NEW BUSINESS FOR KAZOULIS COMMUNICATIONS

2 CHAIRMAN'S SPEECH _____ CLEAR SIGNAL TO COMPETITORS

3 KAZOULIS _____ COSTS BY CLOSING REGIONAL OFFICES

4 'KAZOULIS _____ CLIENTS' NEEDS MORE EFFECTIVELY THAN EVER,' CHAIRMAN TELLS SHAREHOLDERS

5 KAZOULIS _____ RULES ON ADVERTISING: QUESTIONS IN PARLIAMENT

6 KAZOULIS _____ BIG RISK WITH LATEST SHARE ISSUE

7

KAZOULIS _____ SMALL PROFIT IN
FOURTH QUARTER

8

KAZOULIS BOARD _____ DECISION TO
CLOSE REGIONAL OFFICES: MANY JOBS LOST

9

MANAGEMENT _____ AGREEMENT WITH UNIONS
ON NEW PAY AND CONDITIONS FOR KAZOULIS WORKFORCE

10

KAZOULIS _____ LEADING ROLE IN
ADVERTISING STANDARDS CAMPAIGN

11

KAZOULIS _____ NEW PRODUCT
IN YOUTH MARKET

12

CHAIRMAN _____ MAJOR CONTRACT
WITH THE CHINESE

13

KAZOULIS _____ MARKET SHARE
AFTER CHINESE DEAL

13 Business adjectives and nouns

Some adjectives typically go with certain nouns. Complete the letter using the adjectives in the box.

> accurate   competitive   critical   easy   future   guaranteed   high
> large   ~~loyal~~   mixed   positive   right   valued   verbal

---

I.N.Sanebury plc
1 Nottingham Road
Derby DE1 3AB
Tel: 01322 55887
Fax: 01322 55888
e-mail: enquiry@insane.co.uk

Fatima Jones
Frescos Business Services
Bethlehem House
Zelda Road
London
W3 6HJ

Dear Fatima

I am writing to you to thank you for another year of fruitful co-operation between our two companies. You are one of our most (1) _____*loyal*_____ and (2) _____ customers and we always try to give you as (3) _____ a level of service as possible at an extremely (4) _____ price. We are sure that this is the (5) _____ approach.

This is why we want you to be one of the first to know about our plans to improve our (6) _____ prospects through

---

expansion. We have already invested a (7) _____ sum of money in up-to-date distribution facilities and negotiations for further financing are now entering a (8) _____ stage.

The result of all this will be (9) _____ ordering, more (10) _____ figures on the status of your orders, and (11) _____ satisfaction for all.

Of course, there has been a (12) _____ reaction from some of our newer customers, but I am sure that you will be patient with us during the period of transition.

These changes will make a (13) _____ contribution to our continuing partnership and I can assure you that we shall continue to operate by (14) _____ agreement on telephoned orders in the future as we have in the past.

Please contact me if you need more information.

With best regards

Alfredo McKay

Alfredo McKay
Customer Relations Manager
I.N. Sanebury

Other useful adjectives for business are:
customized, committed, entrepreneurial, curious, effective, balanced, flexible
Which words do they go with?
How could you use them in your work?

14 Business adverbs

Insert adverbs from the box into the extracts from business documents or conversations (1–11). There is more than one possible answer for sentences 2 and 8.

> absolutely   actively   ~~conveniently~~   deeply   extensively   financially
> highly   satisfactorily   tactfully   totally   unfairly

1   The new offices are _conveniently_ situated close to the motorway and to the local railway station.

2   I think what he said was unnecessary, inaccurate and _____ unjustified.

3   The new model has been _____ tested and you will be impressed by its quiet operation, ease of use and elegant appearance.

4   She said she had been _____ dismissed but the court said her employer had been right to sack her.

5   Now that the special project has been _____ completed, we can all get on with our old jobs again.

6   Dear Sir / Madam, I am _____ seeking employment and wonder whether you have any vacancies in your accounts department at the moment.

7   I think we should drop this project right now because I just don't believe that it's _____ viable.

8   Your performance in this office over the last two or three months has been _____ unsatisfactory.

9   I think the best thing you can do in the circumstances is to _____ decline the offer.

10   This book is _____ recommended for anyone interested in the workings of international financial markets.

11   ~Are you sure?   ~I'm _____ certain.

15 Business prepositions

Supply the missing preposition(s) in each sentence. You can use some of them more than once.

| at | between | by | in | into | on | to | over | under |

1 Could you call back later? She's ____*on*____ the other phone.

2 It's not surprising that he's working less hard. He's very close _____ retirement.

3 They thought everything was _____ control until they had a big dispute _____ pay.

4 There's clearly a strong link _____ pay and productivity.

5 The people on the shop floor want more participation _____ the decision-making process.

6 We need a much stronger focus _____ the needs of our customers.

7 These meetings always start late. Could everyone make an effort to arrive _____ time next time?

8 I've divided this talk _____ three main parts.

9 It's impossible to say _____ this stage _____ the negotiation whether or not we will reach an agreement.

10 We have to have all the figures _____ the end of the month _____ the very latest.

11 We plan to achieve a 20% reduction _____ the workforce in the next two years.

12 I'm afraid she's not here – she's _____ holiday until next Monday.

16 Business word building

Fill in the missing words in the table.

	Verb	Person noun	General noun	Adjective
1	administer		administration	
2				distributive
3	advise			
4		constructor		
5	innovate			
6	pay			
7			inspection	– – –
8		promoter		
9	co-ordinate			– – –
10			supervision	
11			finance	

The person who pays is the payer. We use this most to talk about **slow payers**. But what do you call the person who receives the payment? Learning a new word often means learning not just one word but several. For example, a person who can **solve** problems (verb), is a good **problem-solver** (person noun). Problem-solvers are good at finding **solutions** (general noun). They believe that every problem is **soluble** (adjective). Building word families like this is a useful and important technique for developing your business vocabulary.

17 Business sectors

Match the companies (1–23) with their sectors (a–w).

1	A company which makes aspirin.	a	automotive
2	A company which mines diamonds.	b	construction
3	A company which makes men's suits.	c	consumer electronics
4	A company which sells package holidays.	d	financial services
5	A company which makes trucks.	e	confectionery
6	A company which distributes electricity.	f	software
7	A supermarket chain.	g	telecommunica-tions
8	A company which builds houses.	h	media
9	A company which makes washing machines.	i	pharmaceuticals
10	A company which sells hamburgers.	j	beverages
11	A company which makes camcorders.	k	textiles
12	An airline.	l	toiletries
13	A company which makes fighter planes.	m	real estate
14	A company which makes shampoo.	n	transport
15	A restaurant chain.	o	utilities
16	A newspaper publisher.	p	household goods
17	A company which sells things over the internet.	q	retail
18	A company which makes mobile phones.	r	fast food
19	A company which sells investment advice.	s	catering
20	A company which makes chocolate.	t	defence
21	A company which makes beer.	u	e-commerce
22	A property company.	v	tourism
23	A company which writes computer programs.	w	extractive

18 Production

Plentiparts Inc. has been having production problems. Unscramble the words in capitals to make sense of the Production Manager's report.

1   At the beginning of the month we were O _P E R A T I N_ G
    quite normally.   (PRITENOAG)

2   There was plenty of S _ _ _ E
    C _ _ _ _ _ _ Y.   (PREAS TPIYCAAC)

3   We had just I _ _ _ _ _ _ _ D some
    sophisticated new equipment.   (LATSLENDI)

4   These were R _ _ _ _ _ S for the main
    A _ _ _ _ _ _ Y   L _ _ E.
                                    (SBOORT) (SYBLMASE NEIL)

5   Unfortunately, a problem developed with
    one of our main S _ _ _ _ _ _ _ S.   (PURLIPESS)

6   They were our only source for a vital
    C _ _ _ _ _ _ _ T.   (EMCPOTNON)

7   Normally they worked very well within our
    J _ _ _-_ _-_ _ _ E system.   (STUJ-NI-EMTI)

8   They could usually send an O _ _ _ R
    within 24 hours of our telephoning for a
    new C _ _ _ _ _ _ _ _ _T.
                                    (RERDO) (GECNINMOSTN)

9   On this particular day, the D _ _ _ _ _ _ Y
    was late.   (VILERYDE)

10 At the same time, there was a problem on
one of the C _ _ _ _ _ _ R B _ _ _ S.

(ROYVENOC STELB)

11 The S _ _ _ _ _Y M _ _ _ _ _ _ R was
out to lunch. (FEASTY ARMGENA)

12 The Q _ _ _ _ _ _Y M _ _ _ _ _ _ R
was away for the day. (LYTAUQI GRANAME)

13 No one reprogrammed the robots, and we
ended up with a lot of F _ _ _ _ _ Y G _ _ _ S.

(LUYTAF SODGO)

'We're having a few production problems...'

19 Marketing

Match the marketing terms (1–15) with their definitions (a–o).

1	marketing	*g*
2	niche	___
3	brochure	___
4	hype	___
5	brand	___
6	upmarket	___
7	downmarket	___
8	sponsorship	___
9	crowded market	___
10	campaign	___
11	reposition	___
12	pitch	___
13	mailshot	___
14	merchandising	___
15	endorsement	___

A crowded market.

a Change the image of a product or service.

b Aiming at the mass end of the market.

c A range of minor products which all carry the name of a major product.

d Aiming at the luxury end of the market.

e A promotional activity over a specific period of time.

f When a famous person recommends a product in an advertisement.

g Matching what the business organization produces with what customers want.

h Promoting a product or service with exaggerated or intensive publicity.

i A small, specialized part of a market.

j A product which can be recognized by its name.

k When the same letter is sent to a large number of possible buyers.

l Supporting a cultural or sporting enterprise in return for advertising.

m One with too many competing products.

n A booklet giving information about the company's products or services.

o What the sales rep says to the potential customer.

Letters which you get about products and services which you haven't asked for and probably don't want are called **junk mail**.

Use the terms in this test to define the marketing strategy of your company.

Do you occupy a **niche**?

Are you in a **crowded market**?

Have you **repositioned** any of your products recently?

20 Human resources

Generosity Inc. has decided to improve the working conditions of its employees. Choose the correct term for each aspect of its new policy. You can then compare the HR policies of your company with the policies of Generosity.

1   We will increase the amount of __maternity leave__ for women who are expecting babies.
    a) maternal leave   b) mothering leave
    c) maternity time   (d) maternity leave

2   We will increase the size of the _____ by 10%.
    a) manpower   b) workforce
    c) human resources   d) employees

3   We will give everyone _____ training at least twice a year.
    a) in-house   b) tailoring
    c) designed   d) outhouse

4   Night-_____ workers will get paid double time for working unsocial hours.
    a) owl   b) shift
    c) time   d) group

5   There will be no more annual _____ interviews.
    a) superior   b) appraisal
    c) objective   d) holiday

6   We will pay everyone an extra _____ at Christmas.
    a) salary   b) expense
    c) commission   d) bonus

7   We will give _____ employees the same status as full-timers.
    a) small time   b) part-time
    c) short time   d) extra time

8   Employees will only have to give one week's ____ before leaving.
    a) notice   b) delay
    c) note   d) resignation

9 No one will be _____ without the full agreement of the union.
a) laid up   b) laid off
c) laid by   d) laid aside

10 Any future reductions in staff will be achieved only by _____ .
a) natural tendencies   b) wasting away
c) natural wasting   d) natural wastage

11 We will reduce the number of working _____ of all employees.
a) years   b) months
c) weeks   d) hours

12 Generous _____ allowances will be paid when the company moves to a site in the provinces.
a) restoration   b) restitution
c) relocation   d) refurbishment

21 Trade

Your company makes spare parts for industrial machines, which you sell abroad. Use the words in the box to complete the description of how you get the goods to your foreign customers.

> acknowledges   bills of lading   cargo   cleared   consignment
> container   customs authorities   delivery   delivery date
> destination   distributor   export   forwarding agent   import
> letter of credit   ~~places~~   port of arrival   sea freight
> shipping documents   warehouse

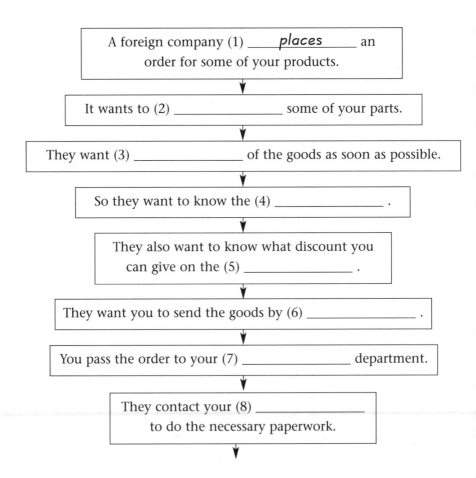

A foreign company (1) ___*places*___ an order for some of your products.

↓

It wants to (2) _____ some of your parts.

↓

They want (3) _____ of the goods as soon as possible.

↓

So they want to know the (4) _____ .

↓

They also want to know what discount you can give on the (5) _____ .

↓

They want you to send the goods by (6) _____ .

↓

You pass the order to your (7) _____ department.

↓

They contact your (8) _____ to do the necessary paperwork.

↓

You do not have a (9) _____ in the country where your customer is based.

↓

So you write to your bank to open a (10) _____ .

↓

You send copies of all the (11) _____ to the bank.

↓

These include copies of the (12) _____ .

↓

Your (13) _____ manager puts the goods into a (14) _____ .

↓

This forms part of the ship's (15) _____ .

↓

The ship takes the goods to the (16) _____ closest to their final (17) _____ .

↓

Here the consignment is checked by the (18) _____ .

↓

Once they have been (19) _____ , they can go on to the customer.

↓

Finally, your customer (20) _____ receipt of the goods.

Some of the shipping terms used in foreign trade are:

CF: cost of freight

CIF: cost, insurance and freight

FAS: free alongside ship

FOB: free on board

22 Finance

Complete the headlines from the financial press using the words in the box.

BANKRUPT   BUYOUT   CHARGES   CURRENCY   DEBT   ~~DIVIDEND~~
FLOW   ISSUE   LOSSES   MARGINS   PROFITS   RATES

1
SHAREHOLDERS
REWARDED WITH
INCREASED _DIVIDEND_
AFTER GOOD RESULTS
AT MEGABUCK

2
MARDOCK GOES
_____ : HUGE
DEBTS UNCOVERED
AFTER POLICE
INVESTIGATION

3
_____
IMPROVE AT
MACROCOMP AFTER
STEEP PRICE RISES

4
JAYBURG FORCED TO
WRITE OFF BAD
_____ AFTER
MAIN SUPPLIER FAILS

5
PRE-TAX
_____
UP AT FLINCO AFTER
IMPROVED TRADING IN
FAR EAST

6
SINGLE EUROPEAN
_____ IS
BOOSTING TRADE,
MINISTER CLAIMS

7
'BANK _____
TOO HIGH,' SAY
NATIONAL BUSINESS
LEADERS

8
'HIGH INTEREST
_____ KILLING
SMALL BUSINESS,' SAYS
MANAGEMENT GURU

9
LONREV ANNOUNCE
BIG SHARE
_____ TO
FINANCE PLANNED
EXPANSION

10
BIGBANK FINANCES
MANAGEMENT
_____ AT
NATBUS

11
NEGATIVE CASH
_____ CREATES
PROBLEMS FOR
PERTH AND STEWART

12
MASSIVE _____
AT GUAM INVESTMENTS
AFTER SOUTH AMERICAN
OPERATION FAILS

23 Facilities

Match each heading (1–12) with the correct description (a–l).

Do the facilities management training course! It tells you everything you wanted to know about facilities management and never dared to ask!

Learn about:

How to:

1 Relocation	_e_	a get the most from machine hire
2 Risk	___	b reduce garbage
3 Health and safety	___	c make your workspaces brighter and better places to work
4 Equipment leasing	___	d provide better canteen services
5 Security	___	e move operations to new sites
6 Recycling	___	f manage real estate
7 Waste management	___	g keep buildings and property safe
8 Catering	___	h reduce accident rates to zero
9 Power management	___	i cut utility costs
10 Refurbishment	___	j draw up legally binding agreements with suppliers
11 Property portfolio management	___	k re-use garbage
12 Contracts	___	l assess degrees of uncertainty

The facilities manager is responsible for the maintenance of the physical, environmental and technological facilities of the organization. It is becoming an increasingly strategic role as companies look for ways both to create productive environments and to cut costs.

Facilities managers can also be responsible for:

heating, lighting, flooring and roofing, contract cleaning, furniture, hygiene.

24 Problem pairs

These pairs of words often cause problems. Choose the correct alternative for each.

1　SUBSIDY / SUBSIDIARY

a) Kazoulis Communications is losing money and wants the government to give it a ___*subsidy*___ .

b) Our head office is in Boston and we own 70% of a manufacturing ___*subsidiary*___ in Colorado.

2　POLICY / POLITICS

a) Rimbaud has been sacked! People are saying he's a victim of internal _____.

b) If we want to convince the public that we care for the environment, we need to change our _____ on dumping waste into the local river.

3　ECONOMIC / ECONOMICS

a) She studied _____ at university and is now an economist with a big international bank.

b) She analyses the general _____ problems faced by companies operating within traditional industries like shipbuilding.

4　ECONOMY / ECONOMIES

a) Their government is trying to liberalize the _____ while keeping tight political control.

b) Overheads are out of control and we need to make major _____ across the business.

5　NOTE / NOTICE

a) He left a _____ on my desk saying he would be late for the meeting.

b) He put a _____ on the board in the main corridor saying that the meeting had been postponed to 3 o'clock.

6 MORAL / MORALE

a) _____ has been at rock bottom ever since they announced the job cuts.

b) When a company sacks such a huge number of people, it's not just an economic question; it becomes a _____ question as well.

7 SAFETY / SECURITY

a) The _____ officer has just been round the site with his dog, checking all the locks and cameras.

b) The _____ officer insists on all employees wearing the right kinds of protective clothing at all times.

8 TAKE OVER / OVERTAKE

a) They want to _____ our company but I don't think their offer is high enough for our shareholders to sell.

b) They expect to _____ all their main competitors, in terms of sales, within a year of the launch of their new product.

'The safety officer said that we had to wear protective clothing.'

25 Word families

Which is the odd one out in each of these groups of business words
and phrases?

1   a) sack   b) dismiss   c) demote   d) fire

2   a) check   b) survey   c) control   d) monitor

3   a) predict   b) forecast   c) anticipate   d) analyse

4   a) lay off   b) employ   c) take on   d) recruit

5   a) rewrite   b) redraft   c) reword   d) restore

6   a) timetable   b) diary   c) schedule   d) strategy

7   a) banned   b) prohibited   c) postponed   d) forbidden

8   a) cancel   b) put off   c) put back   d) postpone

9   a) busy   b) engaged   c) tied up   d) unavailable

10 a) You're welcome   b) Not at all

    c) It was a pleasure   d) Excuse me

11 a) Yours sincerely   b) Yours faithfully

    c) Yours truly   d) Regards

'I'm sorry, Mr Smith is completely tied up at the moment.'

26 Opposites

Each of the words in the box is the opposite of an underlined word. Complete each sentence with the correct word.

> ~~cons~~   contract   decline   fall   fire   lay off
> loss   peripheral   reduce   sell off   weaknesses   withdraw

1 We have to debate the <u>pros</u> and _____cons_____ of this project before we go ahead with it.

2 Let's look at the <u>strengths</u> and _____ of each application in turn and then we'll draw up a shortlist.

3 We expect a <u>rise</u> in sales next year followed by a steady _____ for two years after that.

4 It's simple: we have to <u>increase</u> our prices and _____ our costs.

5 You can see the general position if you look at the <u>profit</u> and _____ account in front of you.

6 At first we saw the company <u>expand</u> rapidly and successfully. Unfortunately, there was a fall in demand and we were forced to _____ our operations to something approaching our current size.

7 We had managed to <u>deposit</u> quite a large sum of money in our account at the beginning of the month but then we had to _____ it almost immediately.

8 We need to concentrate on our <u>core</u> business and sell off our _____ businesses.

9 It's easier to <u>hire</u> people when times are good than to _____ them when times are hard.

10 I would love to <u>accept</u> your invitation but unfortunately there's been a change of plan and so, with great regret, I'm afraid I shall have to _____ it.

11 Our strategy is to <u>acquire</u> large, inefficient companies and then _____ the more profitable parts.

12 Although we have been able to <u>recruit</u> a handful of skilled workers for our main factory, we have also had to _____ several hundred office staff.

27 Idioms

Below each underlined idiom (1–10) write the letter of the correct meaning (a–j).

a	dangerous situation	f	hide something
b	all the time	g	adopt good tactics
c	do something that has already been done	h	bureaucracy
d	no conditions	i	being discouraging
e	refused to	j	experimental subject

1 They should never have tried to <u>sweep</u> that pollution scandal <u>under the carpet</u>.

_f_

2 That company will go bankrupt if they don't cut some <u>red tape</u>. _____

3 At the end of our presentation, he spent ten minutes <u>pouring cold water on</u> our proposal.

_____

4 The head of research herself agreed to be the <u>guinea pig</u> for the trials on the new drug.

_____

5   We agreed to do exercises every morning but we <u>drew the line at</u> wearing the company uniform. ____

6   We must be very careful about promoting ourselves as an ethical company – we're in a <u>minefield!</u> ____

7   Chivers is going to damage his health – he's been working <u>round the clock</u>. ____

8   It's yours for a million and <u>no strings attached</u>. ____

9   They could get the contract if they <u>play their cards right</u>. ____

10 We don't want to <u>reinvent the wheel</u>. ____

28 Business initials

Write the full forms of these sets of initials. The clues will help you.

1   OHP (for visual aids)

   overhead projector
   _____

2   VCR (for home entertainment)
   _____

3   HQ (the centre of operations)
   _____

4   ROI (what you get back from the money you put into a business)
   _____

5   PC (on your desk)
   _____

6   CEO (top job in the company)
   _____

7   IOU (for debts)
   _____

8   JFK (an airport or a president)
   _____

9   GNP (a measure of national wealth)
   _____

10   DTP (software to produce your own newsletter)
   _____

11   MBA (a managerial qualification)
   _____

12   AGM (a meeting for shareholders)
   _____

13   ISO (a quality benchmark)
   _____

14   VAT (a tax)
   _____

15   FT (a business newspaper)

16   AOB (the last item on the agenda)

17   JIT (a stock management system)

18   USP (what companies and products should have)

19   M & A (when companies join together)

20   SMEs (companies of a certain size)

21   MBO (one way to take over a company)

22   MBWA (your style of leadership?)

23   SWOT (an analytical tool)

24   P & L (tells you how rich the company is)

25   PIN (for your bank and credit cards)

26   NLP (for more effective learning)

27   DVD (for sharper images)

YOUR SCORE

All correct: Why are you learning English? You should be teaching it!

21–26: You know the jargon. Try not to use it too much!

15–20: A good effort. But don't get your **PIN** mixed up with your **VAT**.

9–14: You'll get them all correct next time.

1–8: You'll get them all correct the time after next … won't you?

29 Figures

How do you say the following numbers? Choose the correct options.

1   The year 2005:
     a) twenty hundred and five
     b) two thousand and five
     c) twenty five
     d) twenty hundred five

2    $1 = DM 1.46. The exchange rate is:
     a) one point four six Deutschmarks to the dollar
     b) one forty-six Deutschmarks for a dollar
     c) one dollar equalling Deutschmarks one point four six
     d) one dollar making one four six Deutschmarks

3   The period from about 1994 to about 1996:
     a) the midnineties
     b) the medium nineties
     c) the middling nineties
     d) the midway nineties

4   Seven correct answers in a test of ten items. The result is:
     a) seven over ten right
     b) seven out of ten right
     c) seven on ten right
     d) seven right over ten

5   The dimensions of a rectangle 3 metres in length and 2 metres in
     width:
     a) three for two
     b) three by two
     c) three across two down
     d) three to two

6   The result of an opinion survey:
     a) One of ten people think that...
     b) One in ten people think that...
     c) One to ten people think that...
     d) One over ten people think that...

7   Approximately six:
    a) nearly six
    b) six-ish
    c) sixy
    d) sixer

8   At football, Germany 0, Brazil 0:
    a) Germany oh, Brazil oh
    b) Germany zero, Brazil zero too
    c) Germany nil, Brazil nil
    d) Germany and Brazil love

9   3 cm^3:
    a) three centimetre cubes
    b) three cubic centimetres
    c) three cubed centimetres
    d) three centimetric cubes

10 3:2 as a ratio:
    a) three over two
    b) three under two
    c) three to two
    d) three at two

11 A $10m loan:
    a) a ten-million-dollars loan
    b) a ten-million-dollar loan
    c) a ten millions of dollars loan
    d) a loan of ten million dollar

A **24/7** ('twenty-four seven') **business** is one that operates 24 hours a day, seven days a week.
Remember:
10m is 10 million
10bn is 10 billion
A billion is a thousand million
1½ hours is one and a half hours or an hour and a half (or ninety minutes)
The period from January to June is six months (not half a year)

30 Sexist language

Identify and underline the problems of sexist language in the sentences below and use one of the terms from the box to make each sentence less offensive. You can use two of the terms more than once.

~~appropriate clothes~~	chair	employees	face-to-face
Ms one person	representatives	sales	spokeswoman
staff (verb)	staffing	their	women

1   We expect all our managers to wear <u>suits and ties</u> when on
    company business.   *appropriate clothes*

2   Every executive knows that people will form judgements about
    his company on the basis of his personal behaviour.

3   It is the responsibility of the chairman to ensure that meetings are
    conducted efficiently.

4   A spokesman for the company said that she was convinced that
    the new equal opportunities programme would be a success.

5   The company's manpower needs will continue to grow next year.

6   Nearly all our salesmen are against the proposed changes to the
    bonus system.

7   Men found guilty of sexually harassing employees of the opposite
    sex are liable to dismissal.

8   We have to man the assembly line on a 24-hour basis.

9   We congratulate both Mr Smith and Miss Duffy on their success
    in the recent sales competition.

10 If a customer complains, his complaint should be reported to the
    customer complaints department immediately.

11 You have to be careful what you say round here nowadays. The
    girls in the office downstairs might object.

12 I always thought that Sylvie was the odd man out in that
    department.

13 I think you and I should have a serious man-to-man talk, Janet.

14 We estimate that we need 300 more man hours to complete the
    project.

31 Business problems

Pronto Production is in trouble. Identify the problems by unscrambling the words in capitals.

1 The number of customer C O M P L A I N T S has increased by 300% over the last six months. (SALPNITOMC)

2 Many of these relate to F _ _ _ _ _ Y goods. (TULYFA)

3 And also to goods D _ _ _ _ _ D in transit. (GEMADAD)

4 The unions say this is because of the 30% R _ _ _ _ _ _ _ _ N in the workforce. (TROUNCIDE)

5 People on the shop floor are O _ _ _ _ _ _ _ _ _ _ _ D and can't cope. (OVDECHRETRETS)

6 The press has criticized the recent 75% P _ Y R _ _ _ S for the directors. (YAP SIRES)

7 The head of an overseas subsidiary has been caught trying to B _ _ _ E a government minister. (BERIB)

8 The Finance Director has been accused of I _ _ _ _ _ R D _ _ _ _ _ G. (INDRISE DNIGALE)

9 One of the company's main partners has recently gone B _ _ _ _ _ _ T. (KRAPTUNB)

10 The Finance Director is also having cash flow problems because of S _ _ W P _ _ _ _ S. (WOLS SPYARE)

11 And then, last month, the CEO S _ _ _ _ D the Human Resources Director. (KECDAS)

12 She has decided to sue the company for W _ _ _ _ _ _ _ L D _ _ _ _ _ _ _ _ L. (GURNLOWF SMAILSIDS)

13 Since then, several senior managers have R _ _ _ _ _ _ D. (NISERDEG)

14 M _ _ _ _ E is low. (LEAROM)

15 Yesterday the computer system F _ _ _ _ D. (FLIDEA)

16 The share price has D _ _ _ _ _ D by 70%. (POPDERD)

17 The CEO is R _ _ _ _ _ _ D to be working on a new strategic plan on an island somewhere in the Pacific. (RODURUME)

32 Business principles

Choose the best word to complete the following extracts from a company's mission statement.

1 We believe that business can be a powerful ___*agent*___ for social change.

  (a) agent   b) agency
  c) agenda   d) agreement

2 We affirm the need for moral _____ in business decision-making.

  a) valuation   b) validity
  c) values   d) valediction

3 We have a _____ to shared prosperity.

  a) commission   b) commitment
  c) competence   d) competition

4 Businesses have a role to _____ in improving the lives of all their customers, employees and shareholders.

  a) play   b) have
  c) do   d) make

5 Businesses established in foreign countries should contribute to the social _____ of those countries.

  a) advances   b) advantage
  c) advancement   d) adventurism

6 Businesses should _____ international and domestic rules.

  a) retail   b) restrict
  c) repeat   d) respect

7 Businesses should _____ with each other to promote the progressive liberalization of trade.

  a) corporate   b) co-operate
  c) co-ordinate   d) cope

8 Businesses should _____ and, where possible, improve the environment.

a) deflect   b) insect
c) detect   d) protect

9 Businesses should _____ all their customers fairly in all aspects of their business transactions.

a) treat   b) meet
c) seat   d) repeat

10 Businesses should _____ working conditions that respect each employee's health and dignity.

a) divide   b) confide
c) provide   d) avoid

11 Businesses have a responsibility to _____ relevant information to owners and investors subject only to legal requirements and competitive constraints.

a) open   b) close
c) disclose   d) enclose

12 Businesses should _____ competitive behaviour that demonstrates mutual respect among competitors.

a) promote   b) demote
c) motivate   d) provoke

In some countries, **corruption** can create problems for companies trying to do business there. They either have to pay **bribes** (also called **kickbacks** and **baksheesh**) or risk not winning business.

33 Business clichés

The Chief Executive Officer has had an attack of clichés. Help him translate his speech into plain English by substituting each of the words or phrases in bold type (1–21) with one of the phrases (a–u).

Ladies and gentlemen…

1	I want you to **take on board** a number of important points.	_j_
2	Kazoulis Communications is now **a major player** in the communications industry.	____
3	Our strategic aim is to **grow** the company.	____
4	We always **focus on the big picture**.	____
5	If we see a **window of opportunity**, we go for it.	____
6	We work for lasting relationships with **our business partners**.	____
7	We employ **cutting-edge** technology.	____
8	We want to produce the most **user-friendly** products on the market.	____
9	In our business relationships, we aim to **be proactive** every time.	____
10	We propose only **tailor-made** solutions.	____
11	We never lose sight of **the bottom line**.	____
12	We work hard to get **synergy** between subsidiaries.	____
13	We will not hesitate to **downsize** the organization for maximum efficiency.	____
14	We will use our **war chest** to buy up rivals in the marketplace.	____
15	We will find solutions to business problems even when **we do not have a level playing field**.	____
16	If anyone tries to **move the goalposts** on our commercial agreements…	____
17	…we will **blow the whistle**.	____
18	We aim to become a truly **global** operator.	____
19	But we will also **stick to our knitting**.	____
20	Unfortunately I am not **a number cruncher**.	____
21	So I can only give you **ballpark** figures today.	____

a	cut the workforce of
b	business conditions are unfair
c	have a general view of the situation
d	customized
e	a leading company
f	change the rules (without consultation)
g	worldwide
h	the people we do business with
i	increase the size of
j	understand and accept
k	concentrate on core activities
l	dynamic and productive relationships
m	approximate
n	anticipate needs
o	our basic objective (usually to make a profit)
p	good at figures
q	up-to-date
r	easy-to-use
s	protest at unfair treatment
t	a chance to do business
u	a large amount of readily available cash

All business people use some clichés and jargon but expressions like these lose their impact if you use them too much. Other popular phrases are: **market-driven**, **results-driven**, **client-focused** and **best practice**.
When the CEO talks about *growing the company*, he is using the verb with an object in the same way that gardeners grow flowers. In a business context, 'grow' does not normally take an object. For example, we say:
The company has grown a lot over the last five years.
The market grew (by) 3% last year.

34 Business ratios

We use business ratios to measure the financial health of business organizations. Match the ratios (1–12) with their definitions (a–l).

1	Return on capital	_h_
2	Return on assets	_____
3	Profit margin	_____
4	Asset utilization	_____
5	Sales to fixed assets	_____
6	Current ratio	_____
7	Borrowing ratio	_____
8	Equity gearing	_____
9	Income gearing	_____
10	Profit to wages	_____
11	Return on investment	_____
12	Debt to equity	_____

a pre-interest profit expressed as a percentage of capital employed plus short-term loans

b profit expressed as a ratio in relation to employee remuneration

c sales expressed as a ratio in relation to fixed assets

d long-term loans expressed as a ratio in relation to shareholders' funds

e profit before tax expressed as a percentage of sales

f gross interest paid as a percentage of pre-interest, pre-tax profit

g current assets including quoted investments expressed as a ratio in relation to current liabilities

h profit before tax expressed as a percentage of capital employed

i shareholders' funds expressed as a percentage of total liabilities

j sales expressed as a ratio in relation to total assets

k total debt expressed as a ratio in relation to net worth

l profit before tax expressed as a ratio in relation to total assets

'ROA and ROI are looking better this quarter but the borrowing ratio is still weak.'

35 Business strategy

Match the cornerstones of the company's strategy (1–10) with the descriptions
of what it has decided to do (a–j).

Cornerstones of our strategy are:

1	Acquisition	_g_
2	Merger integration teams	____
3	Strategic alliances	____
4	Strategic planning	____
5	Mission and value statements	____
6	Customer satisfaction measurement	____
7	Benchmarking	____
8	Total quality management	____
9	Re-engineering	____
10	A balanced scorecard	____

'She's following an aggressive acquisition strategy.'

We have decided to:

a produce documents that tell everyone where we want to go and what we stand for.

b work to a wide range of performance measures.

c adopt ISO 9000 standards.

d do detailed comparisons of the performance of different parts of the organization with that of similar organizations elsewhere.

e prepare systematically for the future.

f form a group of people whose mission is to create a common culture for the new bigger company.

g buy other companies.

h establish joint ventures.

i work for 100% client satisfaction.

j redesign business processes in order to improve productivity.

A **cornerstone** of your strategy is a very important part – a key feature – of your strategy.

ISO is the abbreviation for the **International Organization for Standardization**. Management theories come and go. **Re-engineering** is much less popular today than it was because many companies only got limited benefits from it. Others, like **strategic planning** (used by almost 90% of big US companies) and **benchmarking** (the most popular tool in Europe) continue to do well. One secret of success is not to try to use too many!

36 Project management

Put one word from the box into each of the mind maps. The ~ shows where the missing word goes.

| actual | bid | budget | cost | ~~project~~ | quality | risk | run | schedule |

1

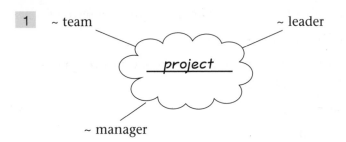

~ team   ~ leader

project

~ manager

2

~ into problems

~ over budget

~ a feasibility study

3

behind ~

ahead of ~

on ~

4

~ assurance

~ control

~ circle

5

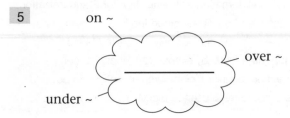

on ~

over ~

under ~

6
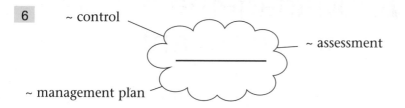
~ control

~ assessment

~ management plan

7
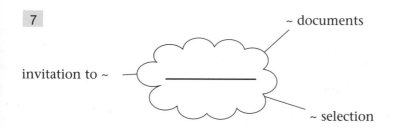
~ documents

invitation to ~

~ selection

8
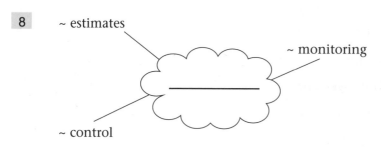
~ estimates

~ monitoring

~ control

9
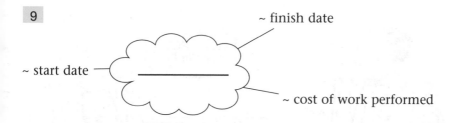
~ finish date

~ start date

~ cost of work performed

People use **mind maps** as a learning tool to remember vocabulary and to brainstorm ideas. In language learning, you can use a mind map to remember which words go together. Put one word (for example a verb, *manage*) in the central circle and then show other words (for example nouns: *project*, *team*) which often go with it. You can then add adjectives that go with the nouns (for example, *difficult*, *challenging*) and so on! People with visual memories find mind maps especially helpful.

Key verbs in project management are:

initiate → plan → execute → control → close

37 Management development

Edgar Schwarz's assessment interview has not gone very well. A human resources manager is telling him about the training he needs. Match each type of training (a–j) with the things he needs to learn (1–10).

a	financial management
b	delegation
c	intercultural communication skills
d	communication skills
e	project management
f	team development
g	leadership
h	time management
i	assertiveness training
j	negotiating skills

'We think you need quite a lot of training: about five years' worth, actually.'

You need to learn how to:	You need a course in:
1 work with other people	*f*
2 motivate and direct other people	_____
3 talk to and listen to people better	_____
4 work with people from different countries and backgrounds	_____
5 bargain with business partners	_____
6 increase margins and control costs	_____
7 set budgets, organize schedules and meet deadlines	_____
8 prioritize your work, and not put off important tasks	_____
9 be more ready to stand up to other people	_____
10 give work to your subordinates	_____

Another term for **assessment interview** is **appraisal interview**. If it happens once a year, it is your **annual appraisal interview**. And one where the appraisal is done by people at the same level as you and below you in the organization, as well as by your boss, is called a **360-degree appraisal**.

38 The management conference

Complete the letter to Dr Strupar by choosing the correct word (a, b, c or d) for each of the gaps (1–10).

1
a) keyhole
b) keynote
c) turnkey
d) keyboard

2
a) conference
b) exhibition
c) trade fair
d) party

3
a) seminar
b) workshop
c) session
d) presentation

4
a) Tests
b) Tendencies
c) Trends
d) Subjects

5
a) plenary session
b) whole session
c) big talk
d) split session

6
a) crowd
b) spectators
c) onlookers
d) audience

7
a) commission
b) royalty
c) fee
d) pay

8
a) aids
b) equipment
c) material
d) helps

9
a) pavilion
b) shop
c) stand
d) floor

10
a) market
b) fair
c) forum
d) exhibition

Dear Dr Strupar,

We would like you to be the (1) _____ speaker at our next international management (2) _____. We would like you to make a forty-minute (3) _____ on the subject of (4) _____ in International Management in the Twenty-first Century. This will be the subject of the (5) _____ which will open this annual five-day event. The (6) _____ will be composed largely of senior managers and management consultants. We should like to propose a (7) _____ of $2,000 for your talk plus expenses.

If you are happy to accept, I should be grateful if you would let me know what (8) _____ you will need for your talk. In addition, I am pleased to be able to offer your company, Strupar Consultants, a discounted rate for a (9) _____ in the conference (10) _____.

I hope you will be able to accept our invitation and I look forward to hearing from you soon.

Yours sincerely,

Jerry A. Poborsky

Jerry A. Poborsky
Secretary General, Association of International Executives

39 Presentations 1

Suzy Capra wants to give a good presentation so she has made a list of some of the things she wants to say. Unfortunately she has dropped all her language cards (a–j) on the floor. Help her to put them in the right order by matching them with the cues (1–10).

Cues

1	Give SUBJECT of presentation.	_i_
2	QUESTIONS OK.	_____
3	LEAD INTO Part 1: History.	_____
4	SUMMARIZE and close Part 1.	_____
5	LINK to Part 2: Options.	_____
6	VISUAL AID: show figures (transparency).	_____
7	Summarize and CLOSE Part 2.	_____
8	MOVE ON to Part 3: Recommendations.	_____
9	CLOSE.	_____
10	INVITE further QUESTIONS.	_____

Language cards

a | Now I'd like to move on to the choices we face today.

b | Let's now move on to the option which I personally...

c | Thank you for your attention.

d | Does anyone have anything to ask or to comment on?

e | Please interrupt if you have anything you'd like to ask.

f | To sum up, the past record of this project is...

g | So let's start with some background information to explain...

h | As you can see, the results are...

i | I want to talk to you today about...

j | That's all I want to say about the current alternatives.

40 Presentations 2

Match the pictures (a–l) with the instructions for making good presentations (1–12).

1	It is important to maintain **eye contact** with the people you are talking to.	_j_
2	Clearly signal the **structure** of your talk during the introduction.	____
3	Select and order your material carefully during the **preparation** stage of your presentation.	____
4	Use the right **body language** to get your message across.	____
5	**Dress** appropriately.	____
6	**Difficult questions** should always be handled politely and diplomatically.	____
7	Establish a positive **relationship with** your **audience** as quickly as possible.	____
8	People will lose interest if you do not move your talk along at a **lively pace**.	____
9	Take a few deep breaths before you start, to help you overcome your initial **nervousness**.	____
10	Use your **voice** effectively and appropriately.	____
11	Make sure your **visual aids** are clear and easy to follow.	____
12	Design and position your **notes** so that you can refer to them easily at all times.	____

a

b

41 Meetings

Match the quotes (a–s) with the statements about the meeting (1–19).

1	Sophie welcomed the participants.	_o_
2	She checked to see who was present.	___
3	She opened the meeting.	___
4	She stated the main objective of the meeting.	___
5	She reminded everyone of how long the meeting was supposed to last.	___
6	She asked Toby if he would make notes during the meeting.	___
7	She invited Sebastian to introduce the first point.	___
8	Naomi strongly supported Sebastian.	___
9	Rebecca made an alternative suggestion.	___
10	Jacob tried to interrupt.	___
11	But Rebecca wouldn't let him.	___
12	Sophie tried to speed the meeting up.	___
13	She obviously felt the discussion was getting away from the main point.	___
14	Sophie invited Jamie to contribute.	___
15	Felix asked Jamie for clarification.	___
16	Sophie summarized the discussion.	___
17	Then she moved the meeting on to the next point.	___
18	Finally, she thanked everyone for coming.	___
19	And she closed the meeting.	___

a   Let me finish.

b   This meeting is scheduled to finish at...

c   Could I just say something?

d   Let's go on to the next item.

e   Let me just go over the main points.

f   It's an absolutely great idea. I couldn't agree more.

g   Is everyone here?

h   We're running short of time.

i   I think we're in danger of getting sidetracked.

j   Could you lead on this one?

k   If I understand you correctly, you're saying that...

l   That's all for today.

m   Could you take the minutes?

n   Yes, but I've got another idea.

o   Thanks to everyone for coming. I hope you didn't have too much trouble getting here.

p   OK, let's make a start.

q   What do you think?

r   The reason we're all here today is to...

s   I'm grateful to you all for your time.

42 Telephoning

The staff of this company are having problems with their prepositions on the telephone. Put the correct preposition in the space after the sentence. Choose from the following words. Some words are used more than once.

back	down	off	on	through	up

1 Just a minute while I look through his number in the company phone book.

look ___*up*___

2 I'm sorry I can't talk to you now. Could I call you down in five minutes?

call _____

3 I'm trying to get off to Mr Schmidt. Could you give me his extension number?

get _____

4 I need to take up his name and number.

take _____

5 Could you hang back a minute while I get a pen?

hang _____

6 I was talking to Mrs Bazin when we were cut up.

cut _____

7 Please could you put me down again?

put _____

8 I've been trying to talk to her all day but every time I call she hangs down.

hangs _____

9 The phone rang and I picked off the receiver straightaway.

picked _____

10 I'm sorry, I don't have this information right now.
Can I get up to you tomorrow?

get _____

Remember, on the telephone:

plan your call

be **positive**

check that the other person understands

KISS: Keep It Short and Simple

43 Socializing

Fit the two halves of each dialogue into the right places in each picture.

A	Thanks for a wonderful evening.		a	So am I.
B	The weather's not too bad today.		b	I'm afraid we got lost a couple of times.
C	Is this your first visit to Rio?		c	No, what's happened?
D	Where exactly do you come from?		d	Better than yesterday.
E	Would you like something to drink?		e	I'm glad you enjoyed it.
F	I hope you didn't have too many problems finding us.		f	Oh, you've probably never heard of it.
G	I'm in Chemicals.		g	Yes, it is.
H	Have you heard the news?		h	Just a glass of water, please.

1

2

3

4

5

6

7

8

44 Letters

Match each of the extracts from business letters (a–k) with the type of letter (1–11) from which it is taken.

1	Letter of invitation	_i_
2	Response to an enquiry	___
3	Letter requesting payment	___
4	Letter of rejection	___
5	Letter of apology	___
6	Letter of enquiry	___
7	Letter of application	___
8	Letter of complaint	___
9	Written warning	___
10	Order	___
11	Reservation	___

a

Mr Kazoulis would like a double room with shower and full board from 12 to 14 September inclusive.

b

I am extremely sorry about the incident last week during the visit of your representative to our offices.
Unfortunately...

c

This is not the first time that this has happened and I must inform you that if it happens again we shall be compelled to issue a formal reprimand.

d

I regret to inform you that your application for the post of Deputy Catering Manager has been unsuccessful. Thank you for...

e

Please find enclosed my CV and a recent photograph.

f

I should be grateful if you would send me more information about your LK range of products including details of prices and discounts.

g

Thank you for your letter of 9 June. Please find enclosed a price list and full details of…

h

Please would you send to the above address 37 units of product reference number 37/LK/45006 (brown) and send the invoice to our West Central office in the usual way.

i

Kazoulis Communications would be pleased to welcome Udo Schmidt to the opening of its new…

j

With reference to outstanding invoice number 9602132/64, we should be grateful if you would settle…

k

I wish to draw your attention to the very poor treatment our representative received when she called on you last week.

45 E-mail

(Match each of these extracts from e-mails (a–l) with the type of message (1–12).

1	Acknowledgement	_c_
2	Request	____
3	Complaint	____
4	Congratulations	____
5	Forwarded message	____
6	Attachment	____
7	Advice	____
8	Deadline	____
9	Apology	____
10	Appointment	____
11	Confirmation	____
12	Thanks	____

a
> Hi Bill, Next Monday is fine, but can we make it 10.30? I have to catch a plane. All the best, Linda.

b
> Bill, Here's the latest version as promised. With best wishes, Linda.

c
> Bill, File received this morning. Best, Linda.

d
> Hi Bill, Could you send copies of the invoices asap. Cheers, Linda.

e
> Dear Bill, Really good of you to see us at such short notice last week. We're all really grateful. With best regards, Linda.

f

> Bill, Next Monday 10.30. Looking forward to it, wbw, Linda.

g

> Bill, This came from Alfredo yesterday. Thought you should see it. Best, Linda.

h

> Dear Bill, It looks good but I think you should sharpen up the beginning a bit. OK? Linda.

i

> Bill, Really sorry. It'll never happen again! Best regards, Linda.

j

> Dear Bill, We've now asked for payment for the last quarter three times. This is not good enough. Please send it soonest. Will call tomorrow if no news, Linda.

k

> Bill, Thanks for the latest section. Whole thing by Monday 9 a.m.? See you, Linda.

l

> Bill, Saw the news on TV this morning. Well done! Thoroughly deserved. Best regards, Linda.

E-mail is increasingly used instead of fax and letters so the style of e-mails can be very similar to that of other forms of business correspondence. E-mails, however, are often less formal than either of the other two. Notice all the different ways that Linda uses to sign off her e-mails. How well do you think she knows Bill? How formal is their working relationship? People sometimes use initials and abbreviations to sign off their e-mails, for example **wbw** for **With best wishes**.

46 Business forms and documents

Name each form using words from the box.

Accident	Application	Appraisal	Attendance
Employment	Expenses	~~Holiday~~	Income Tax
Job	Maternity	Warning

1 I'd like to take a week at Easter and two weeks in July if that's OK.

_____*Holiday*_____ Request

2 Mr Lee had just taken off his regulation cap and gloves when his hair got caught in the machine. _____ Report

3 It tells you about your pay, hours, holidays, pension, and discipline procedures. Statement of Terms of _____

4 The duties attached to this post are as follows…

_____ Description

5 He's been away sick three times already this month.

_____ Record

6 She already has two children and ten years' service so she'll get quite a lot of time off this time. _____ Leave Form

7 There's a vacancy in the IT department which I wouldn't mind trying for.

_____ Form

8 I tell her about how far I think I've achieved my objectives during the past year and she writes it all down and then we talk about next year.

_____ Form

9 He got it for failing to follow instructions and because he broke the health and safety rules. Employee _____ Notice

10 I'm happy to pay for his flight in business class but I don't think we can accept his reasons for staying in a five-star hotel for four nights!

_____ Claim Form

11 You pay more if you're a higher-rate earner and you pay a lot less if you have several dependent children in full-time education.

_____ Return

47 Geography

Kazoulis Communications is an international operation. Choose the correct expressions to describe its different locations.

We have operations in:

1	Birmingham in	(a) the English Midlands	b) Middle England
2	Vienna in	a) Central Europe b) the Centre of Europe	
3	Dresden in	a) East Germany b) the eastern part of Germany	
4	Naples in	a) Southern Italy	b) South of Italy
5	Hong Kong in	a) the Far East	b) Far East
6	Bangkok in	a) South East Asia b) the South Eastern Asia	
7	New Delhi in	a) the Indian continent b) the Indian sub-continent	
8	San Francisco on	a) the West Coast	b) the Western Coast
9	California on	a) the Pacific Edge	b) the Pacific Rim
10	Boston on	a) the Eastern Seaboard	b) the Eastern Coast
11	Iowa City in	a) the Middle West	b) the Mid-West
12	Riyadh in	a) the Mid-East	b) the Middle East
13	Lagos in	a) Western Africa	b) West Africa

We do business:

14	a) throughout the world	b) through all the world
15	a) across all the world	b) all over the world

When referring to what used to be the USSR, you can refer to **Russia** or, if the place is outside Russia, to **the former Soviet Union**.

48 Politics

Match the political statements (1–12) with what people are saying about the government (a–l).

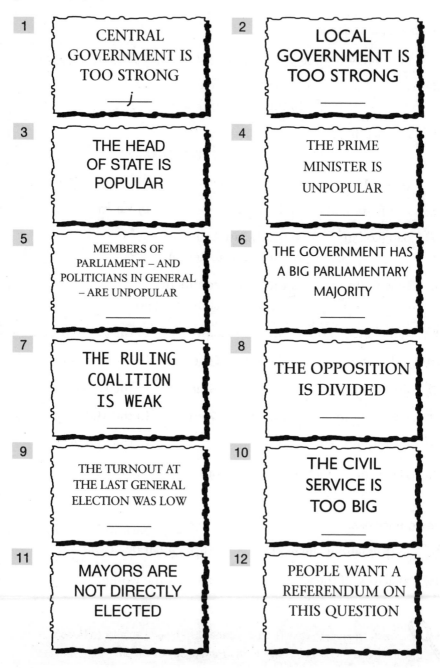

1 CENTRAL GOVERNMENT IS TOO STRONG
—j—

2 LOCAL GOVERNMENT IS TOO STRONG

3 THE HEAD OF STATE IS POPULAR

4 THE PRIME MINISTER IS UNPOPULAR

5 MEMBERS OF PARLIAMENT – AND POLITICIANS IN GENERAL – ARE UNPOPULAR

6 THE GOVERNMENT HAS A BIG PARLIAMENTARY MAJORITY

7 THE RULING COALITION IS WEAK

8 THE OPPOSITION IS DIVIDED

9 THE TURNOUT AT THE LAST GENERAL ELECTION WAS LOW

10 THE CIVIL SERVICE IS TOO BIG

11 MAYORS ARE NOT DIRECTLY ELECTED

12 PEOPLE WANT A REFERENDUM ON THIS QUESTION

a The president is liked by many people, but of course she doesn't have much real power.

b Why can't we choose the city boss directly?

c The government is going to fall if the Social Democrats and the Independent Socialists don't stop arguing all the time.

d The government can always win a vote in the Lower House and so it thinks it can do what it likes.

e The Conservatives and Christian Democrats haven't been in power for ages – and they never will be if they don't stop quarrelling.

f They're all as bad as each other – they're just in it for themselves.

g We should have a direct say on this – it shouldn't be left to the politicians in Parliament to decide.

h I can't be bothered to vote any more: it doesn't make any difference.

i We all thought he was great just after the election, but everyone I know is completely fed up with him now.

j We want power moved away from the big government ministries and away from the capital city.

k There are too many government bureaucrats.

l Our city council can do whatever it likes. The government should have more control over it.

Some countries have strong **central government**, others have a **federal** system, and others have strong **regional government**. The body that administers the smaller part of the country where you live is the **local authority**.

49 The economy

Match what people are saying about the economy (1–14) with what the experts say (a–n).

1 Things seem to be getting a bit better at last – better than last year at any rate. *e*

2 At least prices aren't going up as quickly as they used to.

3 But things are still far too expensive.

4 The problem nowadays is that no one can get a job.

5 The only new factories round here belong to foreigners.

6 The government just won't put any money into business.

7 And even if you do manage to get a job, it's not in a factory.

8 It's more likely to be serving hamburgers in some fast-food place.

9 And either way, the union can't do anything for you.

10 No one's got the qualifications for the jobs you see advertised in the papers.

11 There's no tourism because it's so expensive for people to come here from abroad.

12 I reckon we've got less in the bank than we had a couple of years ago.

13 And now they say we're going to have to start paying to go into hospital.

14 I wouldn't mind a bit taken off my pay if it meant a bit more for schools and hospitals.

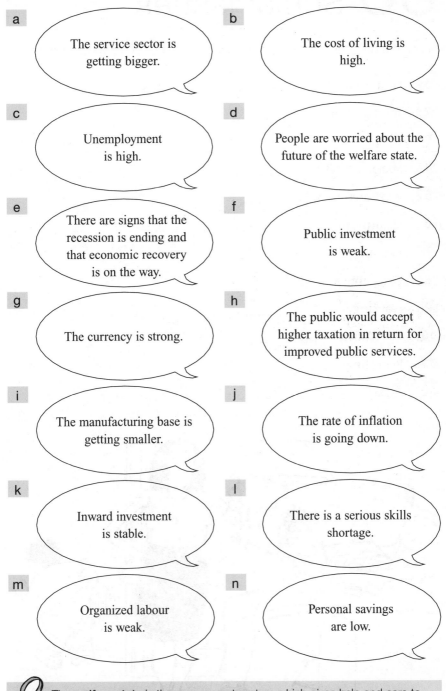

a
The service sector is getting bigger.

b
The cost of living is high.

c
Unemployment is high.

d
People are worried about the future of the welfare state.

e
There are signs that the recession is ending and that economic recovery is on the way.

f
Public investment is weak.

g
The currency is strong.

h
The public would accept higher taxation in return for improved public services.

i
The manufacturing base is getting smaller.

j
The rate of inflation is going down.

k
Inward investment is stable.

l
There is a serious skills shortage.

m
Organized labour is weak.

n
Personal savings are low.

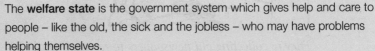

The **welfare state** is the government system which gives help and care to people – like the old, the sick and the jobless – who may have problems helping themselves.

50 Social issues

Match the issues (1–12) with what some people are saying about them (a–l).

1	Homelessness	_g_
2	Immigration	____
3	Law and order	____
4	Social security	____
5	Pensions	____
6	Health care	____
7	Racism	____
8	Drug abuse	____
9	Housing	____
10	Vandalism	____
11	Recycling	____
12	AIDS	____

'They're collecting old newspapers to recycle them.'

a They collect glass and old newspapers once a week.

b There's a twelve-month waiting list for even simple operations.

c You see used needles in the local park.

d I can't live on that when I retire!

e Last night they smashed a bus shelter and a phone box.

f There are too many people trying to come to this country to live.

g We have young people sleeping rough on the streets of our cities. It's a scandal.

h The police should be catching more criminals and the courts should be sending them to prison for longer.

i It's a heterosexual as much as a homosexual problem.

j The government is paying out too much money in welfare benefits.

k The whole estate should be demolished.

l There's a lot of tension between the black and white communities.

51 Travel and transport

Business people often have to talk about how they get around. Match the words and phrases in bold type (1–14) with the pictures (a–n).

1	I was lucky to get a seat in the **carriage**.	_m_
2	Fortunately there was plenty of room in the **buffet car**.	_____
3	The **high-speed train** seemed to get us to the capital in no time.	_____
4	The only hold-up was when the **shuttle bus** to the airport got stuck in heavy traffic.	_____
5	The **jam** soon cleared.	_____
6	The check-in was quick because I only had **hand luggage**.	_____
7	I flew with my favourite **airline** as always.	_____
8	On arrival, I went straight to the car hire desk to collect the **hatchback** I'd booked.	_____
9	It's true I could have had a **saloon** this time since I had so little luggage.	_____
10	As soon as they'd checked my **driving licence**, I was away.	_____
11	Soon I was cruising round the **bypass**.	_____
12	There was a short queue at the **toll station**.	_____
13	But it wasn't long before I was inside the **ring road** heading for the centre.	_____
14	The hotel was just on the edge of the city's main **pedestrianized area**.	_____

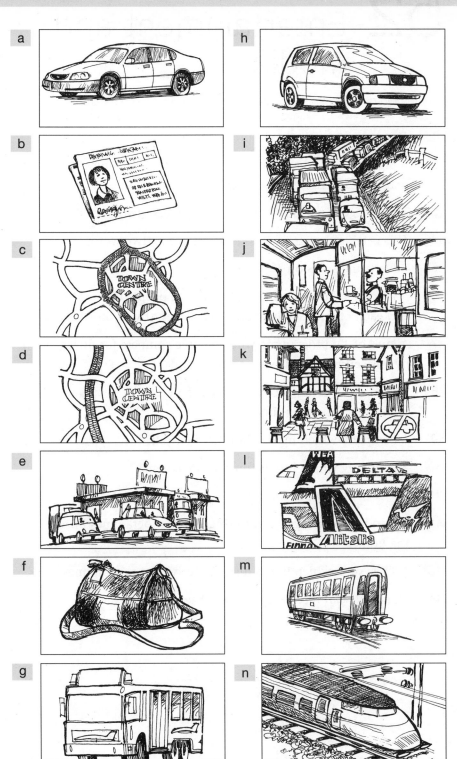

52 Entertainment and media

Find the words in the word square on the next page which mean:

1   To send out a radio or TV programme.

2   A big media company possibly with TV as well as newspaper and magazine interests. (two words)

3   This category refers to popular newspapers. (two words)

4   This category refers to serious newspapers. (two words)

5   Advertising spots on TV.

6   A kind of TV programme where famous people talk to the host and each other, usually about themselves. (two words)

7   A kind of TV programme where people compete for prizes, often by answering quiz questions. (two words)

8   A kind of TV series about the lives of a group of people which often runs for a long time.

9   A company which makes films is often called this.

10   A company which brings films to the cinema.

11   The American word for film.

12   An underground system for bringing TV programmes into the home.

13   A TV system which uses a dish to receive the programmes.

14   Many TVs can receive up to 50 of these now.

The answers read vertically, horizontally and diagonally.

X	V	L	D	I	S	T	R	I	B	U	T	O	R	I	D	S	P	J	B
S	S	M	E	F	H	O	O	L	G	O	J	M	N	I	O	B	O	C	B
T	T	F	D	I	N	E	T	U	V	K	I	C	S	N	C	A	P	A	M
G	C	U	T	O	N	G	A	J	W	Q	O	K	A	D	L	C	Q	W	P
B	H	A	D	E	A	P	B	U	F	U	P	X	T	B	O	R	V	S	I
I	R	S	R	I	T	I	L	P	E	A	F	Q	E	N	L	O	J	A	M
M	A	C	I	N	O	B	O	D	E	L	Z	L	L	R	I	E	D	K	O
E	W	O	R	R	Q	U	I	A	D	I	G	K	L	Y	Q	Y	R	X	V
D	O	T	A	N	S	B	D	M	A	T	H	G	I	H	S	Z	X	L	I
I	P	F	O	J	E	H	P	O	C	Y	A	J	T	T	F	E	S	Y	E
A	U	R	G	I	K	R	R	Q	E	P	C	B	E	F	G	U	W	N	A
E	L	V	C	E	E	D	E	A	B	R	D	I	J	Z	A	V	M	V	H
M	I	H	H	N	T	Y	S	C	H	E	E	C	H	A	N	N	E	L	S
P	V	J	A	B	A	W	S	P	A	S	H	F	U	V	T	B	U	M	L
I	E	N	T	W	R	E	W	W	A	S	Y	B	C	Z	S	C	T	W	J
R	R	S	S	U	M	E	M	F	C	O	M	M	E	R	C	I	A	L	S
E	E	N	H	L	T	E	N	O	N	E	X	U	P	H	Q	T	S	D	X
U	B	R	O	A	D	C	A	S	T	F	O	V	I	T	U	R	Z	I	G
Z	C	O	W	Y	D	R	P	J	Z	Y	G	A	M	E	S	H	O	W	K

53 Tax

SECTION 7

Complete each sentence with a word or phrase from the box.

allowance	corporation	deductible	evasion	exile	free
havens	incentives	inheritance	inspector	progressive	
	~~rate~~	relief	return	value added	

1   The standard _____*rate*_____ of income tax in my country is 25% but well-off people pay more.

2   Marbock has been sent to prison for tax _____ . He didn't pay any tax for five years.

3   In my country, tax on income is _____ : rich people pay a bigger percentage of their income than poor people.

4   I have to fill in my tax _____ before the end of the week.

5   Some of the items you can see here are tax- _____ so you don't have to pay any tax on them at all.

6   You have to pay almost 20% _____ tax on things like perfume, alcohol and petrol.

7   We have been told that we will shortly receive a visit from the tax _____ who plans to look at all our accounts for the last three years.

8   The Bahamas and the Channel Islands are two popular tax _____ because taxes are low so that foreigners who want to pay less tax invest there.

9   The government is keen for foreign businesses to come to this region and therefore gives them a lot of tax _____.

10 These businesses are given a number of other tax _____ as well.

11 The government has increased the rate of _____ tax we have to pay so the net profit for the business is likely to be down next year.

12 He could have received a lot of money after his father's death but he was badly advised and the state took nearly all of it in _____ tax.

13 He earns so much money and taxes are so high in his own country that his accountants have advised him to move abroad and become a tax _____ .

14 I pay less tax than other people because I have a big family and there is a generous state tax _____ for this.

15 She has to wear special clothes for her job but she gets some of the money back from the government because they are tax-_____ items.

In the US, the *tax year* runs from 1 July to 30 June. In the UK, it runs from 6 April to 5 April!
Another term for a **tax incentive** is a **tax break**.

54 The internet

Match the terms (1–16) with the definitions (a–p).

1	Internet Service Provider (ISP)	_i_	9	Online	___
2	Search engine	___	10	Download	___
3	ISDN	___	11	Upgrade	___
4	Bookmark	___	12	Browser	___
5	Hyperlink	___	13	Homepage	___
6	Spam	___	14	Intranet	___
7	Newsgroup	___	15	Freeware	___
8	Keyword	___	16	Virus	___

a an internet application for an internal company network

b a high-speed telephone connection

c bring up to date

d add to a list of favourite website addresses which you keep for easy access

e junk e-mail

f damaging software instructions that enter your computer secretly and can change or destroy information on it

g a link from an e-mail to a web page, accessed by clicking on it

h a virtual location where people can talk and read about a subject of common interest

i a company which gives you an account and access to the internet

j a tool which helps you find things on the Web

k what you enter in a search engine

l when you are connected

m copy information to your computer from another

n a program like Internet Explorer which allows your computer to download documents from the World Wide Web

o the first page on a website

p software you don't pay for

55 Customer service

What do customers appreciate? What do companies aim to provide?
Complete the customer-friendly adjectives below.

1	F A S T	service
2	E _ S _	payment conditions
3	G _ N _ R _ U _	discounts
4	F _ I _ N _ L _	sales staff
5	H _ L _ F _ L	answers
6	E _ T _ A	performance
7	R _ P _ D	response
8	C _ N _ I _ T _ N _	quality
9	C _ M _ E _ I _ I _ E	prices
10	A _ S _ L _ T _	guarantees
11	L _ N _ - L _ S _ I _ G	products
12	C _ E _ R	instructions
13	F _ E _	delivery
14	C _ E _ P	insurance
15	T _ T _ L	efficiency
16	O _ E _	dialogue
17	P _ R _ O _ A _	treatment
18	U _ - T _ - D _ T _	information

56 Business culture

Can you communicate successfully across cultures? Match the statements (a–k) with the parameters (1–11) which help us to understand other national and corporate cultures.

1	Employee relations	*b*
2	Monochronic/polychronic cultures	____
3	Gender	____
4	Titles	____
5	Body language	____
6	Punctuality	____
7	Organizational hierarchy	____
8	Leadership	____
9	Humour	____
10	Time	____
11	Directness/indirectness of communication	____

'I'm happy to do several things at the same time … I think!'

a   If a meeting is supposed to start at 9 o'clock, then I think it should start at 9 o'clock.

b   Managers and unions? It's them and us. You'll never get the two sides to really work together.

c   Everyone calls each other by their first names and I can walk into the office of anyone in the company.

d   If I told a joke at the start of a presentation, people would think I was not serious about my job.

e   I don't like people I don't know to stand too close to me.

f   Just because someone has a doctorate, they don't have to insist that everyone calls them Doctor.

g   I think it's right for the boss to have another pay rise. After all, he takes the risks and the difficult decisions.

h   I like to say exactly what I think and I expect other people to do the same.

i   I tried to help one of the girls in the office into her coat and she got really angry!

j   I tried to call this guy in Norway at 3 o'clock on Friday afternoon and everyone in the office had gone home!

k   I like to do one thing at a time. I can't stand people who start taking phone calls in the middle of meetings.

The ability to communicate successfully across different cultures – national, corporate, professional – is becoming more and more important in business today.

57 Learning

Victoria Snape takes learning seriously. Match the different parts of her learning programme (1–11) with what she does (a–k).

The components of Victoria's learning programme are:

1	Learner autonomy	_g_
2	Emotional intelligence	____
3	Auditory learning	____
4	Lateral thinking	____
5	Neuro-Linguistic Programming (NLP)	____
6	Focus on the competency gap	____
7	Distance learning	____
8	Accelerated learning	____
9	Graduation from the corporate university	____
10	Lifelong learning	____
11	Awareness of multiple intelligences	____

Victoria:

a   thinks about her performance, analyses it and models it on good examples.

b   tries to learn more, faster.

c   does intensive training at the company's main training centre.

d   plans on continuing learning throughout her career.

e   tries to find original solutions to problems by making unusual mental connections.

f   develops the affective as well as the intellectual side of her personality.

g   aims to manage her own learning.

h   uses her computer, multimedia and her organization's intranet for learning.

i   understands that she learns effectively when she listens and hears a lot.

j   understands that her intelligence is more linguistic and interpersonal than logical-mathematical.

k   measures the difference between what she can do and what she would like to be able to do.

58 Organization

What should drive the organization of the future? Match the drivers (1–10) with the philosophies (a–j).

1	a learning organization	_h_
2	a knowledge organization	____
3	a people organization	____
4	a change organization	____
5	a diverse organization	____
6	a cost-driven organization	____
7	a customer-driven organization	____
8	a research-driven organization	____
9	an empowered organization	____
10	a virtual organization	____

a   Technical innovation translated into new products brought quickly to market: that's the key to business success.

b   No office, no hierarchy. We work on-line, we sell on-line.

c   I don't need to ask for the authority to do what is best for my customers.

d   Look after the pennies and the pounds will look after themselves.

e   The service we provide for our clients is second to none.

f   The business environment is in a state of permanent transformation.

g   If everyone in the organization is the same, we could all be caught facing the wrong way.

h   We need to train people to be multi-skilled, flexible, ready for anything.

i   Everything of value here is in people's heads. We have to find how people can share this information efficiently.

j   Our employees are our most important asset.

59 Managing yourself

The concepts (1–16) below are about how to manage yourself. Write the letter of each thought (a–p) next to the correct word or phrase.

1	work/life balance	*i*
2	career development	____
3	learning from mistakes	____
4	creativity	____
5	motivation	____
6	recognition	____
7	leadership	____
8	reward	____
9	risk	____
10	flexibility	____
11	satisfaction	____
12	self-esteem	____
13	fun	____
14	time management	____
15	competency development	____
16	vision	____

Some people set personal and professional **targets** or **goals** or **objectives** for themselves when they start their career. Americans sometimes call this a **game plan**.

a   I want people – at least the people whose opinion I value – to tell me when I've done a good job.

b   I have to prioritize my tasks at the start of each day and then work through them.

c   I expect to earn the money I think I deserve for what I do.

d   I need to be able to respect myself in what I do.

e   Life is boring without an element of danger. I want a sense of adventure in my job.

f   I want a job where I can have ideas, invent, design and make things.

g   I want regular training opportunities so that I can go on developing my skills.

h   I have an exciting picture of the future which drives me and which I want to share with my colleagues.

i   My job is important to me but so is my family and my own private life.

j   I want to manage my team successfully.

k   I want to know that there is a future direction and the chance of development in my job.

l   It's important for me to enjoy what I do.

m   The job I'm doing now may not exist in two years' time. I know that I have to adapt to a rapidly changing business environment.

n   I shouldn't worry if I do it wrong sometimes – as long as I try to understand why it went wrong.

o   I need stimulating and interesting tasks – otherwise it's hard to get involved.

p   You should be able to laugh in your job. Work should not always be serious.

60 Business challenges

Here are some of the challenges facing businesses and business people in the twenty-first century. Match each of the challenges (1–12) with one of the groups (a–l).

1	Risk	*i*		7	Communication	____
2	Growth	____		8	Organization	____
3	Emotion	____		9	Environment	____
4	People	____		10	Capital	____
5	Service	____		11	Entrepreneurship	____
6	Globalization	____		12	Technology	____

a	MBWA	suggestion schemes	company intranet
b	loans	savings	share issues
c	empathy	encouragement	expression
d	initiative	non-traditional thinking	commitment
e	retention	recognition	reward
f	organic	acquisition	joint venture
g	virtual	horizontal	project-based
h	miniaturization	networks	connectivity
i	financial volatility	catastrophe	fraud
j	trade liberalization	economies of scale	government relations
k	speed of response	empowerment	customer orientation
l	sustainable development	renewable resources	regulation

Use a dictionary to check the words that you are not sure of.
MBWA is Management By Walking Around.

Answers

Test 1
1 Tell
2 offer
3 achievement
4 good
5 sort
6 strengths, weaknesses
7 know
8 approach
9 get
10 look for
11 motivates
12 work
13 like
14 learn
15 plan

Test 2
1 primary school
2 secondary school
3 applied
4 place, study
5 subject
6 graduated
7 degree
8 stay on
9 higher degree
10 option
11 grant
12 thesis
13 PhD
14 job

Test 3
1 dropped out   7 wrote
2 joined   8 sold
3 promoted   9 bought
4 spent   10 look after/run
5 moved   11 runs/looks after
6 set up   12 take, off

Test 4
1 k   5 d   9 c
2 g   6 e   10 b
3 i   7 j   11 f
4 h   8 a

Test 5
1 –   7 –
2 to   8 on
3 after   9 –
4 with   10 out
5 with   11 –
6 to   12 in

Test 6
1 h   5 i   9 f
2 k   6 j   10 d
3 e   7 a   11 c
4 g   8 b

Test 7
1 plan
2 portable
3 contributory
4 contribution
5 fund
6 lump sum
7 holiday
8 board
9 trustees
10 retire
11 average earnings
12 early retirement
13 bridging
14 brokers

Test 8
1 Personal computer
2 mouse
3 icons
4 point
5 click
6 word processing
7 file
8 menus
9 delete
10 save
11 select
12 copy
13 printer
14 spreadsheet

Test 9

1 b)	5 c)	9 c)
2 b)	6 d)	10 b)
3 d)	7 c)	
4 a)	8 a)	

Test 10

1 open up a market / open a letter
2 put forward a meeting / put a question
3 share prices fall / trees fall down in storms
4 fill in a form / (be) fill(ed) with pride
5 cut down on cigarettes / cut costs
6 lay off workers / lay foundations
7 break bad news (to someone) / break up inefficient companies
8 sell off parts of a company / sell goods at a discount
9 kick yourself / kick off a meeting
10 take on extra staff / take too long
11 pick the best person / a market can pick up
12 bring up a problem at a meeting / bring dynamism to the job
13 carry out duties / carry passengers

Test 11

1 h	6 m	11 b
2 n	7 a	12 d
3 i	8 o	13 e
4 l	9 j	14 g
5 c	10 k	15 f

Test 12

1 GENERATES	8 IMPLEMENTS
2 SENDS	9 REACHES / SIGNS /
3 CUTS	IMPLEMENTS
4 MEETS	10 PLAYS
5 BENDS	11 LAUNCHES
6 RUNS	12 SIGNS
7 MAKES	13 INCREASES

Test 13

1 loyal	8 critical
2 valued	9 easy
3 high	10 accurate
4 competitive	11 guaranteed
5 right	12 mixed
6 future	13 positive
7 large	14 verbal

Test 14

1 conveniently	7 financially
2 totally/absolutely	8 deeply/totally
3 extensively	9 tactfully
4 unfairly	10 highly
5 satisfactorily	11 absolutely
6 actively	

Test 15

1 on	7 on
2 to	8 into
3 under, over	9 at, in
4 between	10 by, at
5 in	11 in
6 on	12 on

Test 16

1 administer, administrator, administration, administrative
2 distribute, distributor, distribution, distributive
3 advise, adviser/advisor, advice, advisory/advisable
4 construct, constructor, construction, constructive
5 innovate, innovator, innovation, innovative
6 pay, payer/payee, payment, payable
7 inspect, inspector, inspection, –
8 promote, promoter, promotion, promotional
9 co-ordinate, co-ordinator, co-ordination, –
10 supervise, supervisor, supervision, supervisory
11 finance, financier, finance, financial

Test 17

1 i	7 q	13 t	19 d
2 w	8 b	14 l	20 e
3 k	9 p	15 s	21 j
4 v	10 r	16 h	22 m
5 a	11 c	17 u	23 f
6 o	12 n	18 g	

Test 18

1 OPERATING
2 SPARE CAPACITY
3 INSTALLED
4 ROBOTS, ASSEMBLY LINE
5 SUPPLIERS

6 COMPONENT
7 JUST-IN-TIME
8 ORDER, CONSIGNMENT
9 DELIVERY
10 CONVEYOR BELTS
11 SAFETY MANAGER
12 QUALITY MANAGER
13 FAULTY GOODS

Test 19

1	g	6	d	11	a
2	i	7	b	12	o
3	n	8	l	13	k
4	h	9	m	14	c
5	j	10	e	15	f

Test 20

1	d)	5	b)	9	b)
2	b)	6	d)	10	d)
3	a)	7	b)	11	d)
4	b)	8	a)	12	c)

Test 21

1 places
2 import
3 delivery
4 delivery date
5 consignment
6 sea freight
7 export
8 forwarding agent
9 distributor
10 letter of credit
11 shipping documents
12 bills of lading
13 warehouse
14 container
15 cargo
16 port of arrival
17 destination
18 customs authorities
19 cleared
20 acknowledges

Test 22

1	DIVIDEND	7	CHARGES
2	BANKRUPT	8	RATES
3	MARGINS	9	ISSUE
4	DEBT	10	BUYOUT
5	PROFITS	11	FLOW
6	CURRENCY	12	LOSSES

Test 23

1	e	5	g	9	i
2	l	6	k	10	c
3	h	7	b	11	f
4	a	8	d	12	j

Test 24

1 a) subsidy, b) subsidiary
2 a) politics, b) policy
3 a) economics, b) economic
4 a) economy, b) economies
5 a) note, b) notice
6 a) morale, b) moral
7 a) security, b) safety
8 a) take over, b) overtake

Test 25

1	c)	5	d)	9	b)
2	b)	6	d)	10	d)
3	d)	7	c)	11	d)
4	a)	8	a)		

Test 26

1	cons	7	withdraw
2	weaknesses	8	peripheral
3	fall	9	fire
4	reduce	10	decline
5	loss	11	sell off
6	contract	12	lay off

Test 27

1	f	5	e	9	g
2	h	6	a	10	c
3	i	7	b		
4	j	8	d		

Test 28

1 overhead projector
2 video cassette recorder
3 headquarters
4 return on investment
5 personal computer
6 Chief Executive Officer
7 I owe you
8 John Fitzgerald Kennedy
9 Gross National Product
10 desktop publishing
11 Master of Business Administration
12 Annual General Meeting
13 International Organization for
   Standardization
14 Value Added Tax

15 *Financial Times*
16 any other business
17 Just-In-Time
18 Unique Selling Proposition
19 Mergers and Acquisitions
20 Small and Medium-sized
   Enterprises
21 management buyout
22 Management By Walking Around
23 Strengths, Weaknesses,
   Opportunities, Threats
24 Profit and Loss
25 Personal Identification Number
26 Neuro-Linguistic Programming
27 Digital Versatile Disk

Test 29

1 b)	5 b)	9 b)
2 a)	6 b)	10 c)
3 a)	7 b)	11 b)
4 b)	8 c)	

Test 30

1 'appropriate clothes' instead of 'suits and ties'
2 'All executives know...' and 'their' instead of 'his' (twice)
3 'chair' instead of 'chairman'
4 'spokeswoman' instead of 'spokesman'
5 'staffing' instead of 'manpower'
6 'sales representatives' instead of 'salesmen'
7 'Employees' instead of 'Men'
8 'staff' instead of 'man'
9 'Ms' instead of 'Miss'
10 'their' instead of 'his' ('If customers complain...')
11 'women' instead of 'girls'
12 'one' instead of 'man'
13 'face-to-face' instead of 'man-to-man'
14 'person' instead of 'man'

Test 31

1 COMPLAINTS
2 FAULTY
3 DAMAGED
4 REDUCTION
5 OVERSTRETCHED
6 PAY RISES
7 BRIBE
8 INSIDER DEALING
9 BANKRUPT
10 SLOW PAYERS
11 SACKED
12 WRONGFUL DISMISSAL
13 RESIGNED
14 MORALE
15 FAILED
16 DROPPED
17 RUMOURED

Test 32

1 a)	4 a)	7 b)	10 c)
2 c)	5 c)	8 d)	11 c)
3 b)	6 d)	9 a)	12 a)

Test 33

1 j	7 q	13 a	19 k
2 e	8 r	14 u	20 p
3 i	9 n	15 b	21 m
4 c	10 d	16 f	
5 t	11 o	17 s	
6 h	12 l	18 g	

Test 34

1 h	4 j	7 k	10 b
2 l	5 c	8 i	11 a
3 e	6 g	9 f	12 d

Test 35

1 g	5 a	9 j
2 f	6 i	10 b
3 h	7 d	
4 e	8 c	

Test 36

1 project	6 risk	
2 run	7 bid	
3 schedule	8 cost	
4 quality	9 actual	
5 budget		

Test 37

1 f	5 j	9 i
2 g	6 a	10 b
3 d	7 e	
4 c	8 h	

Test 38

1 b)	5 a)	9 c)
2 a)	6 d)	10 d)
3 d)	7 c)	
4 c)	8 b)	

Test 39

1 i	5 a	9 c
2 e	6 h	10 d
3 g	7 j	
4 f	8 b	

Test 40

1 j	5 b	9 c
2 f	6 l	10 g
3 a	7 e	11 i
4 h	8 k	12 d

Test 41

1 o	6 m	11 a	16 e
2 g	7 j	12 h	17 d
3 p	8 f	13 i	18 s
4 r	9 n	14 q	19 l
5 b	10 c	15 k	

Test 42

1 up	6 off
2 back	7 through
3 through	8 up
4 down	9 up
5 on	10 back

Test 43

1 G a	5 B d
2 E h	6 D f
3 F b	7 A e
4 H c	8 C g

Test 44

1 i	5 b	9 c
2 g	6 f	10 h
3 j	7 e	11 a
4 d	8 k	

Test 45

1 c	5 g	9 i
2 d	6 b	10 a
3 j	7 h	11 f
4 l	8 k	12 e

Test 46

1 Holiday
2 Accident
3 Employment
4 Job
5 Attendance
6 Maternity
7 Application
8 Appraisal
9 Warning
10 Expenses
11 Income Tax

Test 47

1 a)	6 a)	11 b)
2 a)	7 b)	12 b)
3 b)	8 a)	13 b)
4 a)	9 b)	14 a)
5 a)	10 a)	15 b)

Test 48

1 j	5 f	9 h
2 l	6 d	10 k
3 a	7 c	11 · b
4 i	8 e	12 g

Test 49

1 e	6 f	11 g
2 j	7 i	12 n
3 b	8 a	13 d
4 c	9 m	14 h
5 k	10 l	

Test 50

1 g	5 d	9 k
2 f	6 b	10 e
3 h	7 l	11 a
4 j	8 c	12 i

Test 51

1 m	6 f	11 d
2 j	7 l	12 e
3 n	8 h	13 c
4 g	9 a	14 k
5 i	10 b	

Test 52

See page 100

1 BROADCAST	8 SOAP
2 MEDIA EMPIRE	9 STUDIO
3 TABLOID PRESS	10 DISTRIBUTOR
4 QUALITY PRESS	11 MOVIE
5 COMMERCIALS	12 CABLE
6 CHAT SHOW	13 SATELLITE
7 GAME SHOW	14 CHANNELS

Test 53

1 rate	9 relief
2 evasion	10 incentives
3 progressive	11 corporation
4 return	12 inheritance
5 free	13 exile
6 value added	14 allowance
7 inspector	15 deductible
8 havens	

Test 52

```
X V L D I S T R I B U T O R I D S P J B
S S M E F H O O L G O J M N I O B O C B
T T F D I N E T U V K I C S N C A P A M
G C U T O N G A J W Q O K A D L C Q W P
B H A E A P B U F U P X T B O R V S I
I R S R I T I L P E A F Q E N L O J A M
M A C I N O B O D E L Z L L R I E D K O
E W O R R Q U I A D I G K L Y Q Y R X V
D O T A N S B D M A T H G I H S Z X L I
I P F O J E H P O C Y A J T T F E S Y E
A U R G I K R R Q E P C B E F G U W N A
E L V C E E D E A B R D I J Z A V M V H
M I H H N T Y S C H E E C H A N N E L S
P V J A B A W S P A S H F U V T B U M L
I E N T W R E W W A S Y B C Z S C T W J
R R S S U M E M F C O M M E R C I A L S
E E N H L T E N O N E X U P H Q T S D X
U B R O A D C A S T F O V I T U R Z I G
Z C O W Y D R P J Z Y G A M E S H O W K
```

Test 54

1 i	5 g	9 l	13 o
2 j	6 e	10 m	14 a
3 b	7 h	11 c	15 p
4 d	8 k	12 n	16 f

Test 55

1 FAST	10 ABSOLUTE
2 EASY	11 LONG-LASTING
3 GENEROUS	12 CLEAR
4 FRIENDLY	13 FREE
5 HELPFUL	14 CHEAP
6 EXTRA	15 TOTAL
7 RAPID	16 OPEN
8 CONSISTENT	17 PERSONAL
9 COMPETITIVE	18 UP-TO-DATE

Test 56

1 b	5 e	9 d
2 k	6 a	10 j
3 i	7 c	11 h
4 f	8 g	

Test 57

1 g	5 a	9 c
2 f	6 k	10 d
3 i	7 h	11 j
4 e	8 b	

Test 58

1 h	5 g	9 c
2 i	6 d	10 b
3 j	7 e	
4 f	8 a	

Test 59

1 i	5 o	9 e	13 p
2 k	6 a	10 m	14 b
3 n	7 j	11 l	15 g
4 f	8 c	12 d	16 h

Test 60

1 i	5 k	9 l
2 f	6 j	10 b
3 c	7 a	11 d
4 e	8 g	12 h

Word list

The numbers after the entries are the tests in which they appear.

A
absolute 55
absolutely 14
academic qualifications 2
accelerated learning 57
accept 26
accident 46
accurate 13
achieve 9
achievement 1
acknowledge 21
acknowledgement 45
acquire 26
acquisition 35
actively 14
actual 36
add 11
administration 16
advancement 32
advice 45
advise 16
agent 32
AIDS (acquired immune deficiency syndrome) 50
airline 51
all over the world 47
analyse 25
annual appraisal interview 20, 37
Annual General Meeting (AGM) 28
answer to 5
anticipate 25
any other buiness (AOB) 28
apology 45
application 46
apply 2
appointment 45
appraisal 20, 46
appraisal interview 37
approach 1
appropriate clothes 30
approximately six 29
arrive on time 15
ask someone for clarification 41
assembly line 18

assertiveness training 37
assessment interview 37
asset utilization 34
attachment 45
attendance 46
at the latest 15
at this stage 15
audience 38
auditor 4
auditory learning 57
automotive 17
average earnings 7
awareness of multiple intelligences 57

B
baksheesh 32
balanced 13
balanced scorecard 35
ballpark figures 33
bank manager 4
bankrupt 22, 31
banned 25
benchmarking 35
bends 12
best practice 33
beverages 17
bid 36
bill of lading 21
blow the whistle 33
board 7
body language 40, 56
bonus 20
bookmark 54
borrowing ratio 34
bottom line 33
brand 19
break 10
break up 10
bribe 31, 32
bridging 7
bring 10
bring up 10
broadcast 52
brochure 19
broker 7
browser 54
budget 36
buffet car 51
build 11

busy 25
buy 3
buyout 22
bypass 51
by the end of the month 15

C
cable 52
call back 42
campaign 19
cancel 25
capital 60
career development 59
cargo 21
carriage 51
carry 10
carry out 5, 9, 10
catering 17, 23
Central Europe 47
central government 48
chair 30
change jobs 3
change organization 58
channel 52
charge 22
cheap 55
check 25, 41, 42
Chief Executive Officer (CEO) 28
civil engineer 4
civil servant 4
civil service 4, 48
clear 21, 55
click 8
client-focused 33
close 36, 39
close the meeting 41
close to retirement 15
commercial 52
commission 6
commitment 32
committed 13
communication 60
communication skills 37
competency development 59
competitive 13, 55
complaint 31, 45

port of arrival 21
positive 13, 42
postpone 25
pour cold water on 27
power management 23
predict 25
preparation 40
presentation 38
primary school 2
Prime Minister 48
printer 8
proactive 33
problem-solver 16
professional
  qualification 2
professor 4
profit 22, 26
Profit and Loss (P & L)
  26, 28
profit margin 34
profit to wages 34
progressive tax 53
prohibit 25
project 36
project management 37
promote 3, 32
promoter 16
property portfolio
  management 23
pros (advantages) 26
protect 32
provide 32
public investment 49
publisher 4
punctuality 56
put 10
put back 25
put forward 10
put off 25
put through 42

Q

qualification 2
quality 36
quality manager 18
quality press 52
question 39, 40

R

racism 50
rapid 55
rate 22
rate of inflation 49
reach 9, 12
real estate 17
recession 49

recognition 59
recovery 49
recruit 25, 26
recycling 23, 50
redraft 25
red tape 27
reduce 11, 26
reduction in the
  workforce 15, 31
redundancy pay 6
re-engineering 35
referendum 48
refurbishment 23
Regards 25
regional government 48
reinvent the wheel 27
relationship with your
  audience 40
relocation 20, 23
remind 41
rep 4
report to 5
reposition 19
request 45
research-driven
  organization 58
reservation 44
resign 31
resolve 11
respect 32
response to an enquiry
  44
restore 25
results-driven 33
retail 17
retire 6, 7
return on assets (ROA)
  34
return on capital 34
return on investment
  (ROI) 28, 34
reward 59
reword 25
rewrite 25
right 13
ring road 51
rise 26
risk 23, 36, 59, 60
robot 18
round the clock 27
royalty 6
ruling coalition 48
rumoured 31
run 3, 12, 36
Russia 47

S

sack 25, 31
safety 24
safety manager 18
salary 6
sales representative 4,
  30
sales to fixed assets 34
saloon 51
satellite 52
satisfaction 59
satisfactorily 14
save 8
schedule 25, 36
sea freight 21
search engine 54
secondary school 2
security 23, 24
select 8
self-esteem 59
sell 3, 10
sell off 10, 26
send 12
service 60
service sector 49
set up 3
seven out of ten right
  29
shift 20
shipping document 21
shuttle bus 51
sign 12
skills shortage 49
slow payer 16, 32
Small and Medium-sized
  Enterprises (SMEs) 28
soap 52
social security 50
software 17
soluble 16
solution 16
solve 16
sort 1
South East Asia 47
Southern Italy 47
spam 54
spare capacity 18
speed up 41
spend 3
spokeswoman 30
sponsorship 19
spreadsheet 8
staff 30
staffing 30
stage in the negotiation
  15